2022 ANTHOLOGY

Aaron Kent is a working-class writer and publisher, and runs the Michael Marks Publishing Award winning press Broken Sleep Books. Aaron was awarded the Awen medal from the Bards of Cornwall for his poetry pamphlet *The Last Hundred.* His work has been praised by Gillian Clarke, J. H. Prynne, Andrew McMillan, Andre Bagoo, Vahni (Anthony Ezekiel) Capildeo, Abdul Kadeer El-Janabi, and John McCullough. His recent books include the full-length collection *Angels the Size of Houses*, and a collaboration with surrealist artist John Welson, *Requiem for Bioluminescence*. His poetry has been translated into Latvian, French, Persian, and Kernewek (Cornish).

Charlie Baylis is from Nottingham. He is the Editor of Anthropocene and the Chief Editorial Advisor to Broken Sleep Books. His poetry has been nominated twice for the Pushcart Prize and once for the Forward Prize. His most recent publication is *Santa Lucía* (Invisible Hand Press).He spends his spare time completely adrift of reality.

Selected Anthologies from Broken Sleep Books

The Plum Review	(2022)
Cornish Modern Poetries	(2022)
Queer Icons: A Queer Bodies anthology	(2022)
Footprints: an anthology of new ecopoetry	(2022)
You have so many machines, Richard: an anthology of Aphex Twin poetry	(2022)
Broken Sleep Books 2021	(2021)
Snackbox: an anthology of Legitimate Snacks	(2021)
Hit Points: an anthology of video game poetry	(2021)
Crossing Lines: an anthology of immigrant poetry	(2021)
Broken Sleep Books 2020	(2020)
Broken Sleep Books 2019	(2019)
Broken Sleep Books 2018	(2018)

2022 Anthology

Edited by:
Aaron Kent & Charlie Baylis

ISBN: 978-1-915079-77-0

Cover designed by Aaron Kent

Edited by Aaron Kent & Charlie Baylis

Typeset by Aaron Kent

Broken Sleep Books Ltd
Rhydwen
Talgarreg
Ceredigion
SA44 4HB

Broken Sleep Books Ltd
Fair View
St Georges Road
Cornwall
PL26 7YH

Contents

POETRY

PROSE

POETRY

January

Dog Walk in the Woods or Jawbone

Premolar 308, 307, 305, canine 304 vulpes
vulpes pulvis et cinis pulvis et cinis canidae
carnivora.

Matriphagy - consumption of the mother by
her offspring
            is a jaw bone.

Parasitic wasps eat their way out of their
stepmothers.
            I'm sure that's not the same thing.
            I'm sure stepmothers would disagree.

A wet snout snuffles at a dry one. The dog
is interested in what I am doing because
            the dog is always interested in what I
am doing.

Restless fox agitated by the rabbit in their
teeth
            308 307
longs for a toothpick.
Just like the witch they'll shovel down dirt
always causing trouble I'll call you kitsune of
the Kentish Downs.   Vulpus invictas.

an archaeologist's plastic nails digging
graves to free the dead. A soiled caesarean
                        section.

Matriphagy or bottle tops that nestle next to
dead teeth, jewels in a crown in coca cola.
E150apremolar 308E150bcanine 304.
Jawbone jutting out of the dirt glacier in a
sun-baked sea.

            You only get to see about 30% or so
            they say. Soon that'll be all that's left.

Spell via Laura's Biscuits

- Take one cup of just enough
- A teaspoon
- Three pinches of happy birthday
- Enough milk to create islands

Disintegrating moth wing page dust. Sit and listen. Still. Listen. Scrape. Scraping. Bone clunks against wood. Dry bones. Desert bones. Dessert bones.

Turgid lumps. Big enough to make a splash. Don't. Lay still. Motion absorbed by the universe's packing material. Wait. Tucked away into quiet caverns. Oscillating stillness.

There is softness to the scraping. Listen. In one ear a hand gropes for something tangible. Falls through like time. Like ants. Scraping. Scuttles up. Like rain at sea.

Valley dwellers all drown. If there were any. Listening. The witch would have been sad. Or paused. At the stop sign spoon with half its head cut off.

Family reunion

Brother of the witch   he is   a
shining glass receptacle,
tanks in human   form
half full to   the middle
of the road a cat with patches of
          water
swilling around   it
dripping and leaking   fur
potential of a childhood
          swallowed by the gulp-full
          drain
draining
unprepared, as we are for the
heat of the sun
          bulb
bulbous
dries
what little water's left
          he is   the fish in
          river
tank
brace ourselves,
against   unnatural waves
walls
          gasping for air
by the   gulp-full
all the while
          drowning
                                    in it

; What we needed was not the same as wanting
but it made for better refusal of unpayable debt
[

; to be forgiven or having received for-giving-ness
much ado in the late spring to mislay a claiming
]

; not to be emptied or excavated by remonstration
had forced a defence of poetry out of the songs
[

; popular calls tort restitution flabbergasted aroma
or it was an arrhythmia apposite to the disclaimer
]

; broader feeling over the sink of realism rose up
alabaster overtures in euromodern surplus good
[

; disgust abound won't surfeit for purpose things
we felt the urge to put our heads through the walls
]

; may've awoken to claret blue dusk in the suburbs
sat on the edge we realised it was not so optimistic
[

; to live in paper and its texture in flight from logic
we became universal individuals by not partaking
]

; in the measure we weren't commiserated or razed
& — we heard each other kicking through the earth –

Might be
          popping out
                    of a break
don't sort it all out   so quick
chained by the hip
          pissed on   ripped steel

through the air like a hiss /
          through the air with a kiss
we broke the door off the hinge
                    & havin' been more
than honest a beer and a spliff
in crystal palace working through
          it subsists on degenerating
                              our flesh into objectives

*

I never learnt because my skin was burnt
          from a rhythm that was in my solar plexus
                    like nerve endings in sinew
to be broken and rebuilt by and with you
I felt reformed or re-issued /now our spines are upright
all the conservatives are uptight
with lips looking like steel girders covered in fireflies
We broke free together ; we were up for the fight
We pissed on the Inglish field;   "it's over like 1979."

</Fuck the analysts> post-lad poly-culture
ready to do sub-fraud origametre
of poems swang like a blade in the z-fold
wrote a big lyric-We:—
told them sad boomers to freshen up freshen up
policemen looking anxious all tense up tense up
spud to the real ones it was all bless up bless up
why you so threatened by us when we á rise up

<end the analysing/> *~~ring the alarm~~*

convinced you an index 'n' middle digit was a hand gun
why you so threatened by us when we just ah hold hands?

[road poetics] not dealt in memoir about brown bugaboos

We won't sell out ~~family~~ for pay we won't work against ~~family~~ again ~~family~~ is extension of affect in the dungeon don't write about ~~family~~ to assimilate. [Revitalisation, yeah] It was summer when we'd fully inhaled. We wrote poems to spread hydration and by the poems of others we were hydrated.

Endurance: Holy Week

for Sarah

A parliament is choiring in her nerves.
   It finds its crises most reliably
at the census-taking. One by one, her doves

   return from the hard country, ecstatically
cooing about a goodlife that persists
   in those abolished regions. She could die

for some good news. An ashen feather drifts
   into her palm, she shivers while it shivers:
blueing and whiting like her blue-white wrists.

   I pity the song of the angelic orders
which inculcates her into downy grief
   for what they made her flesh.
                                                  But her wings' feathers

will be hewn of rich, enduring stuff,
   of kevlar-diamond; which become the smile,
which is the resurrection and the life.

Lucre

I dreamed about the inventory of Rembrandt
the bankrupt's house.
How everything was costed (even the Porcellis)
because he was in debt.
We can't, he says,
understand,
less settle the whole estate
with light ripped from another artist's mind.

Today I can remember Amsterdam,
its wine traders,
and the exotic names of its even its poorest burghers,
because in the worst dream
that night conjures,
she belongs,
not here but in its time,
is living always among Rembrandt's things.

Why do I dream her into that low brown,
that canal light?
It is something to do with the weird,
erotic nature of debt and of things we own,
how the freight
of that whole crime
cannot be told or shown,
as if to tell were somehow to redeem.

The Ship of Theseus

Each night was the same, or seemed to be
a mirror of its ancestors, only
the casks a little emptier at closing
until new stock came in. One day the brassy
handle on the gents began to lose
some of its lustre. Nothing much at first
but after a while the sort of touch the landlord
didn't care for. so he got a new one.
After that the red paint on the walls
began to chip and scuff and darken slowly
until I saw the tannins in its wine.
They gave the place a lick of paint and no one
spoke of it again. But things kept going,
and after that moved noticeably quickly.
First the wear on the tables disappeared,
the red upholstery lost its stench of wind,
and every day the windows let more light in.
The beers turned over at unlikely speeds
and were changed like for like. Once I was sure
that the paintings on the walls had been replaced
by perfect copies of themselves, made over.
The punters never seemed to age at all.
Each year they were refreshed. The same clothes
and familiar names having the same conversations,
those dying generations at the bar.
One August night, I noticed that the clock
was striking eleven again: then I knew
that I had never been inside that pub.
I used to drink in The Ship of Theseus.

one of the main problems with being alive

is that other people accept you more than yourself

this specific thing makes me go into the corner

& bang my head

it's okay Cai they say

but stop banging your head

& I say what you really mean when you say that

is you want me to bang my head even harder

if you didn't then you wouldn't have said the opposite

that's when they look baffled & upset

& say I don't understand come & sit with me

okay

then we hug but it doesn't feel like a hug should

it feels like a very bad piece of wood forever

there's a mosquito rubbing itself into the living room window

in the evening sun

mostly what I contemplate

is where the next headswoon is coming from

& by that I don't mean weed or wine

but perhaps the swan

bossing its way through Venice now the boats've gone

22/4/20

today's the day I release the photos of my burial mound

made of disposable lighters pilfered from the artist

nervous at the doors to the space

lighters

& a sheaf of part stuck collages

lighters

collages

& a Friday night of half cut colleagues whipping themselves

into soft peaks

this morning I found a pair of Oreo doughnuts in a box

with a see through top

perched on a gate post at the front of my house

I took them in immediately

it was too dangerous

5/5/20

Fred Seidel says too much is not enough

Chris Tucker says follow the rich white man

I say I'm high all the time which is both

double rainbow guy didn't need drugs

he just needed a double rainbow

RIP double rainbow guy

RIP Ty

no-one ever really dies

someone said Piers Morgan

shouting at the Tory MP on the TV made him cry

I don't know what to think but the magnesium

a poem made from stardust burns in the dark

nooks of a padlocked academy

it was lit by the ghost of the teacher who marked so many

essays one Sunday

their entire body was repurposed

for the automatic door in the sky

12/5/20

February

The Red Child

I knew a boy whose parents gave him a white rat for his thirteenth birthday. The poor thing was blind, stinky and heavily pregnant. The boy was disgusted. He was hoping for a dirt bike. After she gave birth, the boy would rattle the cage to startle the nursing rat. Then he encouraged me to watch her kill and eat the babies. I remember dark pink slime dangled off her whiskers and we laughed so hard because it was strange and sad and because we thought that was love. I'm not sure if the rat sang a horrid gobbling squelching song as she devoured her litter, or whether I made it up after the boy disappeared. Either way, it's haunting me tonight. I'm dashed with sharp flint chippings in the topcoat of my render. Those council grey, chip fat houses. Baby teeth in old cement. Gorgeous, suffering, his eyes.

Three Months Sober (and it's almost Halloween)

The guy next-door thinks he's such a hero for being lonely. When a frightened woman screams for help on our street, he says it's silly what people do for attention. Sometimes I kneel with them in the road and they tell me what hurts as his face floats against the dark glass like a hungry fish. Most recently, I spoke with a woman who told me she used to be a nun. She was sitting under spectral halogen street light surrounded by torn bags full of clothes spilling out like swollen tongues. When the guy next-door came out to check on us, she waved at him and said, 'You must be a very nice man...' he just folded his arms, sniffing the wind for booze. I remember that spreading pool of piss, how it looked as if the ground was opening up beneath her but somehow I managed to make her laugh. After the ambulance took her away my neighbour said helping people like that is the worst thing you can do because they always come back begging to be your friend. He doesn't know that I have been that woman. That I could be that woman for him. Or he could be that woman for me. You can tell he's got money because his garden is stunning with a white dog and fairy lights and spinning metal sculptures. The way he has utilised such limited space kills me every time I go to my daughter's bedroom window and stare straight down. It has this magic atmosphere, like that secret corner at a festival where there's a pretty couch and maybe some water and someone you love is convinced you're never going to die. Looking at my neighbour's garden makes me want to get fucked up in the best possible way. It makes me want to get fucked up in the worst possible way. It makes me want to never have been so fucked up in the first place. He thinks he's such a hero, keeping his shit to himself. His name is also Bob. It's weird: I hate being called Bob but when I talk to myself I say, 'Fucking Hell, Bob.' Of course they come back, they're *supposed* to come back. We are nourished by the haunted. We live in return.

Power Cut

They found Micky's decomposing body under a pile of muddy rags in his lonely bedsit, gross on a yellow mattress, wide eyes staring at the wall. My dad regrets kicking the door down to find Micky like that, his oldest friend, rotting in his famous denim jacket. As for me, I was basically suicidal at the time. I didn't think I could help when mom called to say my dad is broken. She was pacing the living room when I got there, yelling, 'Talk to your son!' I shifted closer to him on the sofa. 'All gone now,' he sighed. 'Micky was the last one.' I tried to think of something to say as his bloodshot gaze switched to a different channel. It was The Dead Friends Show and in this special episode there was a power cut on the outskirts of heaven, Micky was prowling the clouds, and the angels were panicking. My mom hovered in the dim yellow light of the hallway as if that's what she was put on this earth to do. Dad clamped his hand on my arm, gently shaking it. He said, 'I'm sick of going to funerals.' I hugged him. He felt so small and empty without his mates. Mom must have boiled the kettle a million times. It was pissing it down outside. I walked home with a tearstained impression of dad's face on my shirt. For some reason I wanted to preserve it. I tried to shield it from the rain. I spent the whole journey pretending to be someone else. Someone with the power to do something to radically affect the lost and barely living. Someone who could talk to the dead. By the time I got home I had almost forgotten the details of my own life, until I noticed the bin was overflowing and I'd left my chores to fester. Then I remembered everything - our shitty doctors and my shoddy brain, how rotten and chicken soupy they can be, and how, when I was growing up, my dad only ever woke me twice in the middle of the night, and that was when his parents died. When his mother slipped away he came into my room, sobbing like a janitor's mop on my new Ghostbusters jumper, 'My mommy, my mommy...' When grandad passed a few years later he wailed, 'My daddy, my daddy...' Just me and him, in the council house dark. That was a bad year, life-changing trauma and such. I had wooden bunk beds at the time, switching from top to bottom whenever I pleased. I swear the beds would shake for no reason sometimes, rattling the ladder like a Disney skeleton's arms. I heard crispy old witches whispering in the walls as our neighbour, the vampire, burned his piano on the lawn. Every now and then, when his girlfriend kicked him out, Micky would crash at our place. He would take the bottom bunk after a massive piss up. It didn't bother me. He was the only family my dad really had. I wish the old man didn't have to find him like that. He talks about those staring eyes and that awful dead brother smell. It's with deep fondness I recall Micky's grizzled snore disturbing my dreams. And since I couldn't get back to sleep, I would lean carefully over the railings and whisper the secret shame of my young life, knowing full well Micky was too fucked up to remember anything I said.

Each time I enter the retrospective:
quickness, sanguine intensity

                    and for a moment I have
to stop, everyone milling around

me and the art in the middle. Then I lock
in again, a secret

compartment in the heel of a spy's shoe

once the smuggled thing
—a square

                    of mud or gold or
                    toilet paper, white lead

paint (so heavy)—
has been removed.

[

Rauschenberg instructs someone to write
on the back of *Erased de Kooning*
Drawing, "DO NOT REMOVE
DRAWING FROM FRAME / FRAME
IS PART OF DRAWING" which is just that,
a drawing that's been erased—an undrawing.

[

After he, Rauschenberg,
reclaims paper's beforeness,
it sits on the wall—
a scrim bustle scrape smudge
of sound applied behind it
as to a stage being set.

[

A letter from Robert Rauschenberg to the cast of *Open Score* (1966):

This is identification and instructions.

The stage director will direct you to move quietly upstairs
and wait for your entrance. You will enter into the darkness
and wait for cues. This is a continuous piece and your
entrance should be made as quietly and smoothly as possible.

[

Open Score was a large-scale performance piece staged at the Armory as part of a nine-night performance series. The center of the piece was an unchoreographed tennis match between two players. Each tennis racket was wired to sound whenever it made contact with the ball; they sounded like bells in a bell tower—each chime shut off a light until the arena went totally dark. Once darkness was complete, a group of some five-hundred people entered, announced their names, and faced the audience. Their ghost images were caught with infrared cameras (cutting edge technology at the time) and projected onto large screens around the arena: miniature/magnified mirror of the crowd/each ghost respectively, a shadow mimicry.

[

LARGE NUMBERS WILL BE YOUR DIRECTOR.
The activities that must be executed are listed below and should be memorized. <u>*These will not necessarily appear in the order listed.*</u>

Tracing the Night

After the clocks have gone back
she wakes naturally, fast
emptying of dream.

She pushes back the heavier cover,
lifts the blind, and her usual view's
a blur of spherical pixels,

arcing up to the top frame,
roofs and plane trees nebulous
despite the morning brightness.

Each exhalation, each plume
of dream, has drifted, to layer
its print of alveoli on the pane.

Condensed, a night of breaths.
Each twitch, each depth, each gasp,
is made visible for an hour.

A bead of water melts into another:
she inclines, and sips
each slipping drop.

The Voyage Out

After your slow
deliberation,
your incremental
gathering of pace,
after immersed
practice – drawing
watery breaths,
opening your eyes
on red dark –
after inward
concentration
on the growth
of each pleated,
delicate structure,
lungs folded flat,
voice-box airtight,
each gain propelled
by the umbilical pump
delivering oxygen
from belly to belly,
after all this
your chest is compressed
by the tunnel which leads
into cold blue light,
and out of the darkness
you eventually speed,
and all in one breath
you cry out the switch
from water to land
and plunge into air,
the horizon between
your sea and the sky
now available to
your salt-rinsed eyes.

Did You Think You Could Relax?

I am thinking of felling the palm tree,
it nourishes nothing.

Its split trunk shivers beneath
a hairy blanket of matting.

Last year's yellowed spikes direct
drizzle at random angles,

but really what irritates most
is its bloody-mindedness.

Every year a new corona of fronds
brushes the obsolete telephone wire.

Don't tell me it's ornamental.
Don't tell me not to hack.

A lesson in submarine safety at the naval museum

This dry-dock for men who go under, submariners,
pale as ship's biscuits, fond of being swallowed
whole. Inside, I skip through the pressure doors
and you bang your big old head like a bell. We follow
the tour guide around conventional weaponry,
stroke the smooth torpedo tubes, glue our eyes
to the blind periscope. Dad, you're not yet taken
brassy with the drink's metallic tang, and I'm all ears
at how to escape from a stricken sub in the airless
dark, the lungs that drag men back to the surface.

Thirst

you come cold from the sea and i am a wrecked sailor,
licking saltwater pearls from your blue breasts. i am gone
salt-mad with thirst. my mouth wants the sea inside you.
your bright belly is an upturned boat and i am keel-hauled.
i suck air and our ribs catch. i am swollen and salinated cells
heaving. sand becomes glass under heat. silicate shines
in the telescopic sun. i am anemone-eyed at a low tide.
when i am only cracked ears pressed to the cup of your cavities,
then, then, then, i hear your hot heart boom and i am all echo and drift.

Still Life / Second Life / After Life

For Edwin Morgan *Novgorod School*

An amazing experiment
this heart
that beats like a mountain.
Every page a mountain
a rhinoceros horn polished
into precision steel tubes.
My heart laid bare
[*inter lineas latet cor meum*]
like a still life
like a hanged man
breathing again
with a second life
two minutes of resurrection
then an ascension stopped short
like bread baked hard.

Oh, the oxygen still leaking
from the lesion's eye still seeping
no impeding unrequested
never-ending
soiled and bending
under neon lights where halos
hang their laurels
onto IV drips
as mothers scream
and swallow truths
as hard to chew as hospice food
and stumble out of swaying rooms
no medicine improves
and if these walls could talk
they wouldn't
what's to say in awkward tics and tumors
oh, the shame of shaking hands
that cannot grasp unnerving news
in unrelenting lymph nodes
trauma changes shape and nods its odes
they're moving her like furniture
for surgery on busted springs
and on the astral mattress
there's no rest for cuts
it never seams
your rat-a-tat asthmatic lungs
and blood clots cannot upturn root
a kidney stone's throw from the edge
of fate's unruly marching boot.

It's not about the cancer.
It's about not thinking about the cancer.

There are specific words you need to avoid
to not talk about the cancer.

The problem is that most of them are the cancer
but some aren't quite the cancer.

Like when someone says 'cancel'
but it makes you think about the cancer.
So, you spend the entire conversation
constantly reminding yourself
not to think about the cancer

[*it's too late*]

and if I'm mentioning the cancer too much
well, it's been tall and overbearing,
this cancer of a summer.
The 6 foot 2 of it
keeps searching
for the 5 foot 13 of me.

It's not about the cancer.

[*it's too soon*]

It's about not thinking
of the few months before they told you.

When you said you were going nowhere
a little thought   appeared

what if you die, though?

[*tick, tick, tick, tick, tick, tick, tick, boom*]

then you did.

Define inoperable   I thought to myself
while making a noise
  like a miracle cure
in hopes of you infecting you
with something you deserved.

No one gets to die peacefully anymore.
As soon are you're born
they start to build
  the funeral around you.
The world shrinks
until shoulders   touch soil.

There are times when the words we don't use
    hum a chorus too loud to ignore.

In the moments we choose to avoid them
we are nothing
    and so much more.
        A loudness.
        A shrinking.

A campfire rendition
of all that ceases to sing.

II

Mandragora esplanade sic   indecisiveness anemones
pretention presentational   veiled coiled piecrust split
chequered swede offcuts   mussel inkling perseverate
figurative moisten crowed.   jacaranda dinnerplate put.
Duffel dollops mustang win   tinge by flange cringe lead
would have extricated oven   lift eventually why fold
forehead meant down-hill   we'll have none more ink
batter parental diploid chin   fellow adipose lustrous if
ptarmigan lighthouse farm   dioptre treacle purple site
pillbox anchorage coffee as   bollard annoy retard kites
costard cowardice, imbibed   cruised down along lee fed
spurn lemonade disparaged   fermented, pencil battery
burgess crusted morose age   soft preyed sidelight cruet
molehill full merrier harrier   welded linctus litmus lichen
zealous conspicuous neuron   blown over hurled spillway
tidy fried egg-plant reckless   geese binomial magpie lain
dustbin glacier doorstep tin   rival concealment, insidious
crispin profitless surplice fig   astral buccal manganese ace
laburnum toxic grapefruit lit   distraught inept screw first.

IV

Thān known yet over wrist, well have tune out when
            or did even be fair far before life bridge elevenses
like honest cross at first-come lean or mien, in coral
            just by joist share leaf ridge, so homage most-off
would be true to pay oven evident, exchange; indigo
            clover resume to hospice alpine waning star-burst
immerse measure shoulder or crucial courageous fork
            amiss. Act benefit cloud stand over whether rated
retrieval contrails frugal gainful primal voices harness
            if martingale unless ingress amethyst susurrus fore-
taste undenied gusto door jamb advance, attenuate sit
            promise kept, unity in due approbation highbrow at
take-off nephew contended vigorous singular asphodel
            recondite growls, outside on the dogmatic ramparts
catchwords and hypocrisy portentous unctuous quibble
            apatite apathetic coliform. Vitiate appetite slice cost
ostentatious mephitic acrylic exhumation ziggurat lurch
            rescue in queue curlew callow borrowing; burlap pea
nipper curious stitch renewal epitaxy mercurial yarrow
            morrow tipstaff cyder soliloquy, whisper. Minnow bin
chicory laryngeal scimitar tartaric mesmeric indispensed
            butchery caustic roofer batten nailbed at discomfort,
ingested cirque larkspur crwth corrie obfuscation lesion.
            Living by watchfires, all be still as bright, sulcus circus
matchless abrasion remission incautious suited retrograde
            furthest south-west; earnest alias off incus mixolydian
ambuscade, jasper. Pigeon-toed rush furtive listless invite
            autoclave ill mockery hirsute arachnoid cavatina butter
ignorant twitcher sirventes twelfth manganese cormorant
            yellow-rattle bunsen burner, earner sooner revamped
aubergine angelic assertional sanguine polyp ascetic. Punt
            acrobatic federation operatic doorstep foe midges off
edges badge upstarts piglets wager china cupola perfumed.

VII

Minimal availed silent yet foster- child chilled mortified fort
aspect macaroni marooned slit whisk risk-free mortgages
synchronised optic listed pears immodest fancied weaken
arrowroot water-rat consenting integument docetic air-pin,
dank stonecrop white fleck mat recoiled ahead nostril raced
masonry effigies colt; calamine regent tapir forbearance one
feline enteric factitious archway once up-ended albumen lurk
plaintive talon abreast extricate battlements whence forced;
radiant foreign current deplete falchion along together other
coarse worsen buffoon reminds pulpit pipit greeted cushions
bended reindeer crimson vests, entrancement bonnie weed
who'd at hinterlands concentric for far ago outdone condone
plummet pelmet misfit ice-rink wrangle uncle nuclear unfit,
clump tight candle fused insert swallet clinch borrowed meat
georgic infringement mobile bit marble strait or arrow anew
gorget patch toadflax autumnal stabilised coast-guard gurnard
reminded moonstone waivered arabesque bisque if unflinched
porch portion jacinth winched; jewellery, kenosis fleece teems
tourmaline capstan latchet brick boron fumes grease unceasing
bonded at gammon and spinach off grouse lotus gossamer ink
infirm beseech mortise and end tenon turbulence lustrous scop
crossbow brickwork collar-bone notorious avocets nearby twin
in no time, at all limit ignited oat brisket birdsong winsome apply
sailing on by contrivance pruned prunella stockade aubade bide
collar-bone on sanction gnomon mastodon brunette chancellor
interrogated corrugated, methyl thrilling stent deterrent opals
grapevine seasonal optimal whit mordant scant eglantine must
minaret parkin underwing bloom boisterous yet heir apparent.

Labyrinth of Invisible Pathways

In flight
to capture
the darting step,
steely eye of rock
speed steals the night,
fleeting departure,
heart beat haste,
the race is on
the golden tresses
pizzicato at sonata speed

To no avail,
the crimson breasted bird
red rose in sight,
glance beak blisters
no ears to hear
and yet there's fear,
raw tide is thin
no place to hide

The vile in
crescendo call
past stockinged leg,
in flight
the bird full swoop.
Now golden tresses take to wing
and flocking flaunts another day

L'amour a travers les livres

No hesitancy
this page becalmed
in magnet haze
tumble turned
the words escape
star sprinkled
jostling
to nudged thigh,
the petalled white echo elopes
with constant drift
through moss meshed mischief

The sound of heels heals,
awaiting dawn, the star called awake
Crisp esplanade,
the gossamer placater trickles silken fingerprints
and now the ink is moist

L'amour a travers les livres
2015
29 x 20.5

March

remote living

wreck no less this tangle of
bodged saying a masking tape.
nifty. pop suicide. what is
responsibility. conveyor
sparkle of. be
                    spoke each code a welt.
a ballet. the dazzle of. everyone
shooting everyone with phones.
and just as sin-eaters would
go door to door exchanging
their shouldering of
a family's sin for boarding
now lines of desks
with lines of screens
with lines of underpaid
workers 'filtering' content –

busy trauma of a glut
to be the netting.

the water is rising but this island is actually sinking

no we don't sell straws

but we do sell the fact that we don't sell straws as a way of sidestepping ethical commodities in favour of commodifying ethics. generous emptiness. doncaster. taylor swift. erstwhile. if. shaman. turnstile. if. of course. the homeless. choke. bespoke hemp tote-bag. if of course the homeless choke on no change the government. duck house. will choose cremation. great again. the curriculum. i have. dress. knelt. the apocalypse. before. in fairy lights. your packaging in packaging and. and. and. your value meaning just the same. history in tributaries. so i thought i should make contact. my trilobite. this is how i feel i feel like i should let go. shipwreck. this time a radio. we could have. scrubland. hissing. darlington. between each apprehended is a. seismic. actually. scrap that. caddis fly. piracy. holy holy customer service. blonde. hives. derivative. lanyard valentine. rash. kawasaki. the rush of it. call centre. dark atlantic pills. swig. mills. those feet. procrustes. stuffed crust a rash decision.

rationing the rationing and these hands are red and these mountains elope and a toucan is many and needs more substantial roles in contemporary culture but would then be caged and monetised and made to paint its face in the emergency aisle of a hijacked plane as the passengers fight with blunt quips to best capture their captured descent and the clouds are indifferent but begin more and more to muscle with type as below the sea keeps boiling and the plane keeps to schedule in its plummet and the captain announces his allergies and death is another bag of peanuts in an overpriced catalogue of distractions and without warning excluding all of the unheeded warnings that some of us had secretly lived with for centuries like an uncomfortably deferred evacuation of the lower gut that has been rumbling for so long that its noise became the furniture we so shamefully stretched out in and so and so without warning the toucan came home to roost with a severed beak and the plane crash is now a video clicked in boredom as the ocean howls through every window and somehow you still believe that words are all we have as water fills the mouth and in that moment between the urgency for a voice before its sound and of a struggle before it's over is the readying of a way.

and. and. and. and anyway were you picking up the pieces or sitting in the pile. were you crying *landfill* or *loot* as the event took choice from any script. anaphylactic. donkey kong. shock. barrels. and hand it over. the shrimp knew better. the krill. the coral. the algae. the moss. the mosquitos beatific. the tapeworm. the crane fly. the duck.

prow of ship nosing through. a stillborn flock of. this. each polythene gulp the amniotic answerphone. the waiting for. the once had. the trailing. american beauty. the would-be russian elegy for expecting the unexpected item in the bagging area.

this is old. too old. this is white and old. this is how. learning to shift the. lame. karma. oik. what the white I sees as the silt of it all must not take itself to reinscribe clam chowder. the race to slowly see itself balks fragility. waste. lilied brow of hot bothering strains in claims of. to reinforce itself. to clasp at pearls and flags and genes and to reach for a before all this or a back then a when it was a killing dream of chalk. any normative the deviation. say change was talk

resting on the plunder. the museum. the heritage. a vast and milky never was. the upstairs downstairs little island. renovate a fictional past to sell a backwards future. to make great.

to rule the waves. to white a beached whale. flag in the wheezing blowhole. the bbc montage. coldplay's 'fix you'. cetacean asphyxiation sold as triumph. bleach. fireworks. richard curtis.

michelin men grub hosing brick and boot of white oil. spill so white those gasps of delicate. to finally learn instead the opening from a taking up of. space. to listen and read out.

eton circus quaffs media mess. let them eat. fake. eat on. tea. fake. promise how. tan. the remain will. fake. of the. leave. fake the will of the. fake. this country. take. this common. fake. blazing. matchstick men in three-piece suits with tipp-exed roots now selling tailored erasure of their power as it grows and grinning entrepreneur or knowing the. fake the. common man. the bald honk if you're threatened. the turning to. the overspill of anger and fear. white-tac poster boy web intellect posturing. induct. initiate. lost feta blockheads crumbling. online far from any raft. to tell them they are right. of white oil. right to feel anger and fear and to make themselves again in that image because it is right. right if right means hurting for the few

and holding rage you never chose with vulnerability imposed by those who promise they speak on your behalf and spell out exactly how to hate. but what was left was not. smothering so close to. was not without blame. smothering with oil. what squabbling left had left them as a 'them' to the wringing hands of pyramid-schemes-for-the-soul and youtube recruitment. the skin can't breathe and the eyes are all and only white and the ears are closing to all but that spill.

flayed beluga kite a cross a blimp to lift olympic lions wreathed in colours lying and the crown a lord a crime excused by wealth and where victoriana frathouse binds bullingdon cuffs to link dead swine to fuck and undead squealing megaphones wire-up to where the larynx was and now the strung-up carcass shouts to fill a shape of who to hate and raise a pint and promise change while casting eyes from cladding flame clamp ears to cries that still without an answer rise unheard in now and blatant real each voice a bird in smoke that keeps its call alive and calling still and calling now and calling from a burning tower and calling from a burning tower.

I don't write letters much anymore but i used to In the months that followed the sexual assault i had written or rewritten at least fifty letters which i would pretend to send to men i thought were least likely to understand In my letters i tried to convey the things that happened to me hoping to find ways i could make sense of it The first letter i wrote was kind of an apology even though i was still trying to justify what happened still trying to find a good reason for why i had come home you know When i saw the doctor i cried a little When i lied and used my parasomnia to get discharged i cried less After i continued writing trying to craft the most elaborate letters each trying to convince someone that i wasn't insane and i was just a coward who didn't have the courage to report it After a few months i grew frustrated and stopped trying to justify what happened and stopped writing The thing was that i had learned how to survive life in a shell and i had learned to live without sleep I didn't eat well and i stopped playing basketball and started drinking heavily and eventually my partner convinced me to attempt therapy but that was years after and the therapists didn't help at first The first summer i tried to fuck as many people as I could but i was too drunk most of the time and i had no time to write not even letters as i tended to do on the weekends Hallucinations disturbed me nightly of a being that looked like my attacker's father's father and of an abstract shape that moved almost levitated against a wall Waking up from these felt like living as i went straight to wanting to convince myself that what happened hadn't happened I found that i could often pretend that it hadn't happened if i just kept watching too much TV Or read a book I was sick of life so sick of even attempting sleep so tired of screaming and the low moans of the neighbours watching soap operas so clearly i could almost swear they were speaking to me In a strange and desperate attempt to console myself i began writing love letters to men i didn't particularly like Through these i thought if i write enough love letters then someday someone will read them and they will love me and take me away from the noise and the lights and the nightmares and away from the dirt under my nails and i will be free It was wrong i was wrong but it felt so good to write the letters that i could not stop I was sixteen when i first found a man i wanted to fuck I told him to come over and i took a shower When i stepped out of the shower i was completely nude the door was locked and the bed was covered with a comforter so heavy and soft that i could barely move the thing When i reached to grab the blankets my arm was entangled in a large ugly long purple tree frog He had nestled in between my left arm and my right leg which were locked in a sort of claw The frog was fully capable of sinking its spikes into my right leg and i was completely petrified I fell onto the bed trying to get away from the tree frog but i tripped and fell onto the comforter and the tree frog began biting at my arms and legs trying to eat me The more i fought against it the more i became weak and defeated until i had managed to get some of the large bites to form a bloody puss on my right arm The frog was trying to eat me i could not lose I crawled to the door and i threw the door open yelling at the man telling him that i had been bitten by a monster He looked down at me with that odd patient look and said It's not a monster darling And it wasn't but i refused to believe him I refused to believe that the thing that had entered my flat in my bedroom was not a monster In my mind i could see the dirt under my fingernails could see the scars on my inner thigh could see the deep cuts across my chest and i believed that they could belong to something ugly and unnatural As it began to gain momentum i could feel its body become stronger harder more aggressive I tried to hold onto my rational thought but i was losing and the monster was stronger I looked older and i looked older and older I was not a child When i was not a teenager i had been with 4 people in my life 2 men and 2 women but i guess if you include a lack of consent i had been with 5 people in my life 3 men and 2 women I had hallucinations again of a being that looked nothing like him and of an abstract shape that moved almost levitated against a wall In the last years the only time i've written letters has been when I was particularly manic After my diagnosis with Borderline Personality Disorder i wondered if he pushed the illness into me Was BPD sexually transmitted I wanted to write letters about rape I wanted to write letters about mental illness I wanted to write letters about how toxic masculinity is killing us all I wanted to write about killing him again and again and again until i was burned out on the pain and confusion and pain and misery and pain and fury that my youth had left me with and i had no words left I would try to make these letters beautiful to illustrate a sunny side of the darkness that was overwhelming me I thought if i could do that i might gain some small relief from it at least in my mind The difficulty with this approach is that really i was trying to convince myself that i was okay It was an obsessive attempt to reconcile the two sides of myself and a shame-based attempt at recovery Of course there was no simple resolution to my mental illness or my assault but there was something i desperately wanted to believe I wanted to say i had won but i gave up calling myself a survivor or a victim I gave up calling myself on the phone That was a struggle a hard battle an intellectual fight with and between myself and an idea that had taken over my mind and no longer allowed for an honest representation of my trauma Years had passed and my pain had moved I felt like a shadow of my former self diminished in size in consciousness and in my world The monster had started to slowly reassert itself and i would try and force my mouth to say i was okay but it refused to let me It demanded i accept that i was broken that i was not the same guy who had listened to shrimp give a round of applause for a career It demanded that i be a stranger to myself And when i had been on that path for so long the monster had ceased needing a place to rest I gave up on myself I could not hold myself together I felt my body shutting down I went into what i call my minimal autonomy mode where i would be awake and alert and aware but i would almost completely disengage from the world I would have thought that this was why i was still alive But the truth was that i was alive because i did not care enough to kill myself I did not care about myself or my life or the people i loved or my family I did not care what people thought I did not care what people said I could see nothing hear nothing and see no one I would walk around and i would have the sensation that my entire body was turning into a void But if you blinked you would miss me I did not care about myself I did not care about my family or my friends or my students or my cats And i was profoundly lonely horribly lonely My parents would tell me that they cared and my brothers would tell me that they cared but it was a joke that you tell because it makes you feel better I could hear them and see them and their words seemed to do nothing to stop the sunless reality that filled my head I did not know how to care I did not know how to connect I was empty and alone I did not know how to make myself feel better In my mind the assault that i had suffered was now my identity it was who i was I felt worthless broken used My physical self did not matter and i did not care about my body I could not feel safe anywhere but i felt particularly unsafe in the space between my flat and my car I would run a short distance from my flat from the front of the flat and to the car door If i heard a car coming i would run back to my flat As the car drove away i would stare at the spot where it had been I wanted to feel safe but i didn't know how When i drove home i always drove home with my windows down music on full blast even in torrential rain or hail I would stop driving and pull into dead ends and i would just sit in the car inside a car while it was raining outside rocking back and forth I did not have friends or family who understood this they never had because i had not let them I didn't want anyone to understand I didn't want anyone to care about me I didn't want anyone to give a shit If i could tell my attacker about what happened afterward about this aftermath would that make it better Would he think twice Would i be fixed Would i not be a piece of shit Would i be able to move on to heal Revenge would make me feel better revenge would make me feel complete I would wait When i was at my lowest point i was raptured in my seldom sleep as i wondered if my soul was going to slip out my mouth when i swallowed my final breath I imagined telling him all about it hoping that it would bring me comfort like he might have been able to feel me and care and i wouldn't be alone anymore I guess the rapture was too early cause i fell right back down my body like a door being slammed in the face crashed to the ground The night terrors always felt hypnagogic but after an hour i knew i was real and i knew what he did was real and in my pain i really did feel like i was alone even when i was lying in bed with strangers I was alone I was lonely It was incredibly hard at group therapy to broach and deal with what had happened to me I didn't really know how to process it I felt angry and sad I felt confused and lost and scared I felt like i couldn't trust people and i didn't know why I spent the first few weeks really the first few months just trying to navigate the whole survivor thing It's a confusing game to be a survivor There should be someone around you who's your best guess of having done it first

Russian Dolls

Before breasts,
your poetry is peaches

& cream in cornflower dress,
a doll-cask of sweet sap.

Then, the thrum of blood;
you are on the cusp,

your pupils black moons
bringing the tide.

You are a red creature
bound at the wrists by biology,

your poetry is puce and vermilion—
a ripening lacuna lush

for the splitting of cells,
the giving of yourself

to a body
within a body.

A History of Love Letters

Miss said every time I told a lie,
Baby Jesus had a nail hammered
                    into his hand.

She said I had a *sad mouth*,
corners downturned, pointing
                    to hell.

Stephen had a mouth like sunshine.
I gave him a token,
                    a tiny toy dinosaur egg,
                    pale blue and gold.
I wrote his name on my hand and hoped
the egg would hatch.

My body grew and Granny said, *never*
shave your legs—so I did. Better bald
                    spring chicken; better descaled,
plucked bare for boys with nervous fingers
to work me open.

The one who wrote love letters spilled
his entrails in black biro, telling me
                    in no particular order
the parts he liked best—some illustrated.

When Napoleon begged his Josephine to lay
                    herself bare, he meant for her flaws
to fold her into neat and precious squares;
                    for her to be less
than his clenched fist heart could hold.

In place of a filigree pen, my hands
hold pistachios peeping from the lips
of yawning oatmeal shells,
                    ripe and given up easily
for a hungry mouth that isn't my own.

I Want You to Know that You Are Alive

The natural law is that sometimes,
this must hurt. You will find yourself
hurled headlong into a mound of salt,
skin raw, inside out. And you will know, then,
what it means to be the wound—
what it means to learn how to breathe
through it all.
Know that it is a bravery to live
at full capacity; fill each lung
with equal measure of dark and light.
Drink every cup dry.
Know that nothing is ordinary,
and all things are temporary—
we can never outrun this bittersweet truth.
But, a secret: we can stop, for a moment, and taste it,
unafraid of the sting. It's easier
when you know it's coming;
when you lean into the fall, go limp,
and let the cushion of your knowing
absorb the impact. You will heal
again and again, until.
You will.

The Right-Hand Book of Stock Photography

For Dantalion

Hey this wheat
field shimmered
straight to gold status.
Is this how
the ache of empire
operates? When you put
white people in a fever
dream
house it's solar-powered.

It isn't that the stars
have started falling
for our benefit.
It's that location
is for the poor.
This tableau in relief
against Las Vegas
or the Colosseum.
Why not both?
dad asks through
a mouthful of squid ink.

I mean you can either vote
for family values
or drape a Soviet flag
over the lower forty-eight.
See inset for Alaska and
Hawaii.
Having not cracked
geography entirely just yet,
the strategy is to hyperlink
and rain glitter down
quick. The khaki comes
on strong like Charybdis'
puckered asshole watermaw.

Some existences linger on long after the death of the thing itself.

This archive
dislocates my subject.
Each photograph
furnished with p-zombies.
My consciousness clicks
into the slots of their lacks.
This is what I call
a hard problem.
The redness of their wine
shares a redness with mine,
though a screen is nothing
if not equivocal.

Similitude only poses an issue
as long as you address it.
Noumenon, from
Greek νοούμενο,
"to think, to mean."
As in I can grip a kite string
but the ultimate kite
escapes me, in fact
refuses me by its very nature,
the essence shrouded
on the far side of its image,
as are all the people waving.

Negotiations break down
approaching the thing-in-it-
self.
The front end accordions
against what appears
to be horizon.
But of my vessel-objects,
how do all their faces
know to look away?

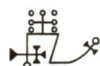

Ghost Opening Its Shirt

For Murmur

Would you do me a kindness
and quit dying on the internet
in front of me? I am petitioning
the gods I believe in:
Ghost ex machina;
ghost opening its shirt
as a metaphor for power;
five hundred and fifty Tiffany lamps
that shatter into the stupid night.
Inheritance powder was
a euphemism for poison
in seventeenth-century France.
Now when Grandpa dies
two people arrive in trench coats

[We cannot be too careful in our choice, for it determines the body we inhabit.]

to shower you with medical debt,
paperwork like cherry blossom petals
raining over a cinematically
recreated cobblestone street.
I am so thankful to be alive
in the U. S. of A.
where our souls have access
to vast lines of credit
taken out in our children's names.
Still, the committee keeps deciding
not to grant an award this year.
All that work for nothing.
Well "yes, and"
is the key to good improv, you know.

Biomassive Black Hole

For Barbatos

The skull wrapped in a red bow
marks where you died
the last time around and the last

Two thousand pounds' worth
of spiders could eat
a two-hundred-pound man in one

Dredging a corner you missed
previously / here is a dog /
here is someone's child / this sewer

When you find everything
you came here for
kneel and let the black wolf

These fox
ears make you
invincible

GREEN CUT MOAT

Round once, and then again, you go,
circling the house like a red pen, marking
out job ads in newspapers. He follows,
our growing friend-child, the veil bearer.
His hair shortens as his height lengthens
and new clothes appear with each loop
of the year. This is you playing grown up.
This is me, laughing, doing the same.
We're becoming real, we are real people,
with cars and houses and lawnmowers that
bandage me in. Inside the house, I sit, my
bruises wrapped like a Christmas present,
smiling every time you hula-hoop with the
noisy grass-eater. Our green cut moat is our
wedding ring, haloing commitment to our
lives, together, like gold leaf to a Bible.

IN THE COMMUNE

The language of politics was my lullaby , my Sufi ascent from the baobab tree to ancestral spirits robbing thoughts, like magpies, eggs, from the living until they too die and rob , my heritage, not of tin roofs and stampeding hooves of poverty of fishing rag-tailed and speaking crêpe creole of de sweet chilli burst of Auntie Mattie's cooking dat scorches memory in blander times in clouded drizzly mid-October bleach , my tales I did not know well enough to entertain or teach with a shimmy and a belly wiggle a breast pop and a jingle of the coins lining my buttocks. The domed twirls of the *ezan* chiming five times a day we abhorred, pillows made of Lenin. My baby-speak was of politics, of marching 8 billion by 8 billion hurrah hurrah! , my fleeting aspiration for animals two by two, mother by father, selfish when here I had multiple honorary guardians, aunts and uncles, and brothers and sisters, where here only the cherry tree paired off fruit to be dangled in duo, from ears that looped the hearsay and buried it deep in the gut. Romantic idealism rocked me to and fro. Nightmares, of innocents imprisoned, their families left to the metronomic bars of the onward tide of dissenters disappeared of rats the size of children of crafts – stitched, weaved and braided – of unwanted rubbish turned into want, for instance, wallets with change locked like their makers for instance, pastel paintings scraped like shit stains. I had not the alluring hot coolness, or did not know enough of it, or cared not to market it, no, I had the ga-gas and the goo-goos of politics unsteady on its feet and of grubby fingers drawing all to the whoops and whooshes of fairground descents.

0 1 1 2 3 5 8

Male mosquitos are said to hum at D natural, while females at G, two of the most common notes in human song, a fifth, part of the triad, as everyday as arm-stretching when waking up yawning, a musical Fibonacci linking us to mosquitos, dolphins and the growth of mushrooms, like the sequential spiral, the snail, shell and the petals of flowers.

April

chimp

A punishment for humans arrives divinely

in the apes.

Chimp don't hear.

Not the sun.

Always at the start of trouble.

Starting trouble for the sun.

Not hearing night.

Chimp only hears the de before the words that contain it.

It calms, chimp chews the wafer handed into its mouth that it was sposed to swallow.

Chimp don't swallow, chimp chews.

Chimp licks a bee like it was a battery.

First finger then middle then ring curls around the nape of the neck.

This is my enemy that was once friend

palm now on the jaw

now gun shot

no other life in the region of hearing can be heard

because palm now on the jaw

be careful a brave tree animal can be saying

get the car, says another.

I don't hear the sentence, I'm just watching

my role as a researcher is to watch

never to intervene.

But the fingers, the palm, the jaw.

Shadows are once hot wax being not so hot

The jaw of this other creature, this once friend now enemy is putrid.

Shakes, tears, calling in to rest no more rest, no more food

Food is blue.

Food is bland.

Food is tubed.

I wipe my orange juice from the carrots.

I hide my children. I barrel into my fence.

Someone else behind me, a human, will not stop talking.

Greasy ribs, electric wires, pearl jam songs, transmissions from the past they are obsessed with,

axes, tallow, beetle, belts, worn on badges, sharp planes.

Camera clicks, really? Now.

Chimp has got jaw for hot mess fear you utter.

Then guesses, a robber, who owns the most popular supermarket? Oh that's it.

Ecological concerns.

We're in the jungle mate. Chimp is elephant.

Chimp is war.

Chimp is noble.

Chimp is award.

Chimp hips are unimaginable to this liar sat behind me in its own fancy shit.

A sky fish will come I hope and tin looks facial features like birds knot themselves to distract

cardio from weights

nutrition from studies

evolution from pork

is it, think Chimp, the pork or the beans that got caught in your zipper?

Chimp drinks iodine and sweats it out for us to recognise it as close to us.

Knocking shoulders, eyebrows, chests. Never before ajaw.

Why did I research myself through Chimp?

No swimming here, no barons, no well to do at all.

The shop is closed, the food damp.

The elephants are cool but their babies rude.

They cross the laps of my girlfriend just to sit down and then where will she?

Where do you vacation? says from behind me.

Americans, I think, think and Chimp might jaw them.

But ugly finds itself.

Green military uniforms become suits

workplaces open,

roads bring transports, children sleep on them.

Phones are and will be.

I want to eat these trees to make the jungle the clear sight

and paper and a football field and a thing to keep me

as I want to live on and that kneeling throbbing

will last briefly

like the baby in the lap of my women

and it'll wink

and wince

REJECTED BY SUBWAY FRANCHISE EMPLOYEES ON 18TH STREET I WALK HOME WITH NOTHING

I admit
she slid the sandwich
onto the counter so
I could have
grabbed it

But $5.99 is too much for a sandwich

If you think about it
that's a dollar an inch

In theory
you can't trust no one
especially me
having the self respect to walk away
if my coupon is not honoured

Do I have to prove I *have* money

Unlike the 3 guys sitting on
the sidewalk outside the store

But I just don't *want* to *use* my money

I'm not pressing submit
on my time-
sensitive coupon just to prove a point

Žižek said freedom is painful
—Co-sign—

Do I literally
have to build an organic social media following
in order to get the coupon
for my sandwich respected

At a pay rate of 12 inches
an hour
minus me having to stay alive

The human condition

I put in work for that coupon

I got 3 people to sign up
for the Subway Club ™ but don't worry about it

I should put some of my other problems
            in this poem

A poet recently told me
            everything is political

Don't you think I wish I could be normal too

Walking home with nothing

String of lightbulbs hung up by the lake edge

Sun setting on the contradictions

Just dark enough to see a body lying on the ground

Just light enough to avoid it

I HAVE THE SWAGGER OF A 17-YEAR-OLD

Overheard in the passage to the L train: a man saying "I'm 28 but I have the swagger of a 17-year-old" over and over

Fucking me is no longer illegal. Everyone I've ever known is still alive. I might be wearing a wig. I just jumped a turnstile. I don't have any tattoos. I just made a mix CD with only one song on it. This shirt is ripped on purpose. Everyone is so bogus and I need to inform you of that. I deliberately misspell notes I write to myself. I have a file called "Masturbation document" on my computer and also my e-mail. I made desktop backgrounds in MS Paint of celebrities telling me not to open it and to go back to doing homework. I'm still really sorry about what I did. I'm trying to work on not telling everyone about it constantly. I wish I was joking, a lot. That's why I say "I wish I was joking," a lot. I think everybody interprets this to mean that I am joking, so it's like a wish that works for everyone except me. I've got that driving-on-a-permit swagger. That tinfoil grill swagger. That food-wrapped-in-a-napkin swagger. I'm crying in the hallway. I'm wearing your T-shirt. I think you wanna date me. I only said that because I saw it in a movie. I actually want to stand in a corner and sing the same song loudly into the wall.

DIRECTIONS TO MY HOME FROM TRAFALGAR SQUARE

I put in headphones and walk into traffic. Imagine the drivers are screaming with desire for me over a horn section. Yeah son, throw that empty water bottle at me. I know what you need. I am dark, infinite, brooding. These guys' pork pie faces are my drum kit. Bash crash bash crash benefits benefits bastard bass. I didn't get smaller. That doesn't happen. I just got outside my body. For once, I'll be the steady one. I put the sound on my back. And if anyone is out there, I'll try again on this channel every Wednesday at noon. Don't let them fool you. It's the same dog as in the advertisement except it's dead and comes in a box. There are infinitely stranger preservatives added to pepperoni than the mind of man can invent. Birth defects aren't funny but they aren't always sad either. If someone had just reminded me that, when measured in potato, fries are the lovemaking and chips are the fucking. But nobody tells you that do they. They just expect you to remember it. Who's that sexless creature who stalks the streets? Only me but I've installed an extra drum behind me for when people ask that exact question. Bon soirée. His fingers have definitely gotten thicker. Not that I'm complaining. Three men sleeping on window ledge of furniture store called Habitat. The store set up to look like a home, lights still on. Many planters of soil. A rustic bench. Art does not require intent or observer. "Lucky to Live Here" cross-stitched on a pillow. Empty. Everyone dead no doubt in a nuclear attack. I lick the dirty sleeping bags, then lick the window. My tongue memorizes the scene. I spit everything out in reverse order. On the train, someone in front of me mentions Rick Ross, then, after a while, adds that a lot of people are probably dying right now. I imagine a centaur composed of Rick Ross's torso and the legs of a thousand corpses. After we disembark, waiting in the road for the crossing gates to lift, a skinny teenager falls in the shadow of his girlfriend and begins to press against her with his hips, as if he is an exclamation point alternating with a question mark. He has been fingering her silently in the seat next to me the entire ride. They are some undulating terror and perhaps we are only allowed that a few times in our lives. It will feel like swinging over a gulch this time, rather than artillery. Please refer to me not by name but only in vignettes. We are almost back now. From where I live, the world is a line of lights strung across a black thicket. That is the airport, and that is London, and that is a rose which in the darkness looks blue, gathering the hedge around it as the heart gathers electricity. To everyone I know, I will be distributing tickets redeemable for one last round of constant apologies while I beg to make out with you. After that it won't happen again. You will be able to remember how it tastes.

Holiday

Initially, to keep from totally losing it, I confess
to subscribing to the notion that this would be over
in three weeks; that we would drop out and use the time
to pick up new skills, bake endless loaves of cider bread
and feast on kitchen cupboard antiques. What can't you do
with a tin of chickpeas? Finally – I can do yoga. Stand
on my head after twenty-one days, the Welsh words
tumbling out like cawl from a ladle, hot splashes
peppering my poems. I saw all this. Bliss.

Santa Cruz Serenade

After Impulse Control *by Rachael Llewellyn*

Take me. To the cinema, to the scene
of the crime, either and. Meet me late
in a terrible nightclub, pass my name back
into my handbag, swap it for another.

Dress it up like suicide in memory
of cookery class with mother, cello lessons
but don't look in the case. The red door, furnace
fit to fuck with you for life. Peroxide

makes me invisible. Unless I'm working
from the warehouse, where I make it look
like an accident that sends a message.
I was a baby at the start, barely a teenager

and now, love. Refined and correct
as possible but I still need a slice,
lie in demon because Amber saw me
drop a head off a pier. Scarlet splash –

hey, I'm not here for spoilers.
Just to administrate, clean knives
and pick the glass fragments. Know
that this can't go on, waiting

for the digitalis to take hold
and the bullet to leave
the chamber. I need
my own terms to live.

Dolphin legend

News spread. A whole pod came
beaking and bottling to break the green,
absence of gondolas. Venice may sink
slowly but that day, dolphins took the virus
to task. The Earth said no. People stood
in awe, blood vessels breaking their links
in their creamy eyes. Retweets began, reposts

filled the marshy foundations of
the transmissions we accept.
The infection justified – a planet holding
back its oppressors, calling no more, let
animals reign. That was the legend.

Truth thinned it down – their blue hides
were photographed in a Sardinian port
hundreds of miles away, relentlessly normally.
This breathless curse is ours and we can't benefit
from a lens pointing at the wrong churn of water.

Notes on what to expect if you're stabbed

As the knife enters your body
Your muscles will contract
And you'll release air like a burst balloon.
There will be a sharp intake of breath,
Your body will stiffen like clay in the sun.

Please remember this:
You will not bleed out like in the movies,
Your shirt will not be dyed in an instant.
Your life will edge off slowly,
Like a prisoner sensitising to light.

Noodle Brain

I finished it twenty minutes before it happened,
Bombay Badboy. Not the last meal
That I had imagined, but who knows
                                        when the end is the end?
What I remember about the drive in the ambulance
Wasn't the pain or procedures, but the thought
That you would get home and find the pot
On the countertop, left out of laziness as usual,
And silently curse me for not doing what you ask.
And I couldn't deal with that curse then,
Not at that moment when I needed you most.
Maybe the reason why I haven't had one since
Is because it looks like a dried-out brain,
And the sudden shock of the hot water stirs
It all to life again,
                              the sachet of sauce
                                        ripped open like a wound.

Aberdeen

Thinking back, it was a mad idea
To go up to that top corner shelf
Of land in such precarious health,
Just four weeks after the stabbing;
My skin a translucent parchment,
My body a bag of broken ornaments.
We didn't appreciate how far
It was that morning we jumped in the car.
But we had to escape the claustrophobia
Of home, the interview the perfect excuse.
Neither of us said but we both knew I hadn't
A chance of getting in: frail, shuffling shade
Of my former self. More junkie than teacher.

Our premonition turning out to be true.

I was morose on the way back home,
Angry, anchored in misery, black clouds.
When you pulled in at Tyrebagger
To empty the car of my weather
I told you to just go, to leave me there,
That you would be better off on your own,
Before the freezing February air,
Lethal on my lung, had me coughing up
Sorrys on the edge of the wood where snowdrops
Had blanked out every inch of the ground,
A clean slate, Spring's latest shot at life,
And you stood next to me, taking my hand,
Telling me that everything would be all right.

In the downpour of your absence

we collect our grief in the pockets
of our eyelids as if it might
let us see you again — if only once —
before the inevitable erosion
of memory; the precise vibrations
your voice made through air
or the particular distorted shape
of your body shadow-cast
on the pavement, tiny cracks
in the architecture of you
we have constructed, cracks
that widen and snap so that we
press our fingers to our eyes,
try to keep you intact
but we cannot stop the dissolving.
Fragments slip down our faces,
clutch at our quivering chins
before slipping silently away.

Margot

She smoked cigarette after
cigarette behind the bike shed
until she disappeared completely
always in white, white dress,
white socks, white shoes, black
cigarettes to match her skin,
small burns on her fingers hidden
by silver rings, white nail-varnish.

I watched her thinking, always her
small face held in a hateful glow.
I hate the feeling but cannot stop.

One night I see her floating above me
in bed, unsmiling. Mr Smith had said
she was hit by a car, that morning
in assembly. I touch her black hair,
her dark mouth, her breast.
At school she had looked at me
with a knowing. I touch her now.
My insides protest.

Family History

They found my body swollen between the arms
of a chair, my acid-burned fingers clutching at the hem of my dress.

My sister embedded in the walls, her hair hanging
from her skull in webs, chest open and heartless.

My brother a wound beneath the bathroom sink,
his blood-shot skin coating silver pipes.

They saw my mother as a sorcerer, the ritual
of muttered hexes, her dowsing crystal still in hand.

On the news they showed our faces, headlines bore
no meaning to who we thought we were, ghosts without voices.

We haunt the hallways, haunt the walls
and the garden as our shadows eclipse the moon.

Our faces rubbed purple with grief, the traces
of us no longer in the architecture of our home.

May

The Fucking Fuckers

You and J are fucking. Although J is on top of you, neither you nor J think that you are the ones *being* fucked (that is, both of you see yourselves as the *fucker* and neither of you see yourselves as the *fuckee*; and that is both of you see yourselves as doing the fucking and neither as receiving it).

It's not that either of you consider yourselves unequal participants; it's more that in order to see yourselves as *any type* of participant in your fucking you would both require a much more analytical sense of mid-fuck scrutiny than either of you two fucking fuckers can care right now to give.

For you, the view of yourself as the fucker is predominately because it has simply never occurred to you that you might not be one; that is, that you might be a *fuckee*, one who *receives* the fucking? No, this is inconceivable. It would be like trying to understand blindness by closing your eyes instead of by studying a picture through your elbow.

For J, however, it is different. J is not above thinking of themselves as a *fuckee* on occasion (and here J is more honest than you, because J will admit to, in the past, having been happily most happily fucked). But J refuses to accept that whether choosing – yes, *choosing* – to become a *fuckee* is determined by anything so arbitrary as mere position. What about when you are both lying on your sides? Or both standing up? Or both draped over a chair like wet coats? Clearly, mere position does not always help discern who it is that's doing the fucking and to whom, and thus what determines someone's status as a *fucker* or a *fuckee* must be something else and, yes, while it's true that, right now and lying on your back, you are being more thrust upon than thrusting, but *you know* it was in fact J who instigated this particular fuck by turning your skin as sharp as bark with a careful brush of a hand and so, if – *if!* – J is now *choosing* to be a fuckee then it is only because J has acquiesced: and acquiescence is born from choice and choice is born from power, and power means, of course, that in J choosing to *not own* the fucking it is in fact J who owns it after all.

So, when J comes with a wet clench and collapses on you like an ironing board, You are tempted – *almost* tempted – to say 'That was so good'.

But you don't – knowing, of course, that saying 'that was *so* good' is really saying: 'please reassure me that you enjoyed that to at least something approaching a similar level as I did and that we are at least on an equivalent plane of fucking and that I am not in a river while you are, say, in a puddle'.

So you don't say anything. But then J rolls over and says, 'That was *so* good'.

You sleep in fitful snatches after that, shallow dreams that break like poppadums, until you find yourself awake once more. The moon is coming in through the curtain, landing on J's face so it's unclear whether J is smiling or dreaming of finding loose change. You pause – then shuffle into J, lick an earlobe, trace down J's thigh with a fingernail. J stirs awake and you whisper through the darkness '*fuck me, fuck me hard*', your words ringing out like a klaxon opening a Black Friday sale.

The Erection Specialist 1

Half-fucking-six he picks you up
in the end. Half-fucking-six,
after telling you to be in Salthill for half-five,

when you 'd called him the day before,
rang the number in The Advertiser:
Erection Specialist Needed

(well now that'd got your attention –
labourers to put up a marquee)

where in Salthill? you'd asked him,
the bit near the sea, he'd said and then hung up.
The bit near the sea.
The bit near the fucking sea.
Ah he'd sicken your hole,
and sure you should've known then.

So there you are, you and a young lad

(Murtagh his name was, you find out,
in the end,
when you read it
in the paper)

and waiting for nearly an hour,
walking laps of a flicketing streetlamp
circling it like a pair a bicycles afraid
ye'll tip over if you stop,

stamping your feet awake in your boots,
blowing billows of breath into cupped-up
hands and dreaming of being buried
back in your beds, but quiet though,
not much chat that hour of the morning,
ye can both tell it's shaping up to be a cunt
of a day, something about it,
the grawness of it maybe,

and you're only ayting through the fags,
one then the other then the other,
nom nom nom
nearly quarter of the box gone
when the sour prick finally screeches
up in the van

(a brand-new Mercedes Sprinter mind,
ah he had no problem spending money
on the van, he looked after that right enough)

and he rolls down the window
and you see his big slab of a head for the first time;
red, bulbous, sweating;
a pure thick-necked prick from out past Gort,
and he's wearing one of those black
Thinsulate caps, like you'd pick up
in a petrol station bargain basket-bucket,
so a brand-new van and the auld fucker
wouldn't even buy himself a proper fucking hat,
I mean that's what you're dealing with here,
and he lets off a snarl at you like a tumour
prolapsing out of a badger's arse:

come on to fuck ye're late. I told ye be up by the hotel.

Well by Christ you know what way it's going now,
you have his jib well and truly cut alright,

but you've been out of the scratcher over an hour
and you think you should at least get paid *something*,
anything, stop the whole morning being a total meowl,
a pure woejus altogether,

so you walk around to the passenger door
and open it up. And what drops out?

A rolled-up marquee wall.
Hits you right on the knee.

Put back that fucking wall and get in the back, says he.

Eight Algorithms For The Self-Driving Self

1. You are driving on a residential street when you are forced to swerve to avoid a van. To your left is a murderer. To your right is a baby.

2. You are travelling through a 50 kmph zone when you are forced to swerve to avoid a truck. To your left is a baby – who will grow up to become an estate agent. To your right are two babies – eating a murderer.

3. You are a zipping along a country lane when you are forced to swerve to avoid a small mountain's solitude. To your left is a text you sent in your twenties. To your right is the one you never could.

4. You are cruising along a motorway when you are forced to swerve to avoid a recently reclassified planet's sense of inadequacy. To your left is a culturally appropriated indigenous votive taking advantage of its now enhanced public profile to exploit lesser and more impressionable effigies. To your right is a Twitterstorm marinating an avocado in beard oil.

5. You are blaring down the Autobahn when you are forced to swerve to avoid the hours invested in the second season of a box-set where the monks break back in to the monastery. To your left are the gargoyled eyes of a final year PhD student who's been asked, but in passing, about her thesis. To your right is a national treasure avoiding tax by fly-tipping a paedophile wearing a poppy.

6. You are careening up (and down, simultaneously) a Penrose staircase when you are forced to swerve to avoid the nights you turned down sex to play the computer. To your left is a marmot still maintaining it voted Brexit to make immigration fairer for non-Europeans. To your right is an echidna espousing literal, but à la carte, adherence to scripture.

7. You are hurtling across a Möbius strip when you are forced to swerve to avoid a monocle wearing a Che Guevara t-shirt. To your left is a burning tower block justifying austerity by conflating national expenditure with a household budget (overlooking, of course, that national expenditure raises revenue in a way domestic spending never can). To your right is a woman who CC'd in your line manager.

8. You are flashing between inter-dimensional wormholes when you are forced to swerve to avoid the difference between popularity and populism. To your left is the entirety of your future contained in the eyeballs of a god. To your right is the entirety of your god contained in your future eyeballs.

How did it start?

The coast
an umbilical cord of closed
mairies and stretches
of unshaved chins open to the sky.

The coast
has seen sickness invading before
boats ruptured far away
off the coast of Cornwall, of England.

The coast
viewed from above is a flat surface
under which hide furious notes.
The coast is a rotary dial and it has been calling.

The coast
draws itself closer everyday,
it's had a good haul.

The sheep
The site picked for the nuclear site
is being controlled by sheep now.
Literal sheep. Not poetry sheep.

The sheep
The sheep are on trial today,
though the court didn't invite them
to defend themselves.

The occupation
Decades after the Nazis, a new force
fills the same buildings, stuffing the courtyards
of the seminaries with their vans.

Comment cela a-t-il commencé ?

La côte
un cordon ombilical
de mairies fermées et une étendue
de mentons mal rasés tournés vers le ciel.

La côte
a déjà vu la maladie envahir
des bateaux se rompre au loin
au large des Cornouailles, en Angleterre.

La côte
vue d'en haut est une surface plane
sous laquelle se cachent de furieuses notes.
La côte est un cadran téléphonique et elle ne cesse d'appeler.

La côte
se rapproche chaque jour,
elle a fait une bonne pêche.

Les moutons
Le site choisi pour la centrale nucléaire
est à présent contrôlé par des moutons.
Des moutons, littéralement. Ce n'est pas une métaphore.

Les moutons
Les moutons sont jugés aujourd'hui,
bien que le tribunal ne les ait pas invités
pour se défendre.

L'occupation
Des années après les nazis, une nouvelle force
s'installe dans les mêmes bâtiments, remplissant les cours
des séminaires avec leurs fourgons.

The occupation
The police come to find posters declaring the start of the survey.
They find none in Plogoff, in Goulien, in Cleden, in Primelin.
So they return, plaster them, take a picture as proof, then vanish.
The posters do not last long on the wall.

The occupation
A helicopter frightens the birds away.
We call her mère-poule, mother-hen.
She covets her riot cops.

The crêpe
Everyone has their trick, but the common method
is to scoop the mixture with a ladle,
place it on a buttered bilig, and rake it into a circle with a rozell.

The crêpe
When the time is right, take your spatula
and slide it under the lace
holding your crêpe over it like a train.

Carefully lay it on its other side, ready to receive.

The crêpe
The first few times you try to make a crêpe,
you will either make holes, or fail to spread the crêpe
fast enough, so that it bottles at one end, slower to cook.

Backstage
It's the eve.

The French flag at half mast, the Gwenn ha du hoisted.
The folders of the survey burned by the four maires.
A white night is coming as the shadows creep up,
the first barricades are sewn.

L'occupation
La police vient chercher les affiches déclarant le début de l'enquête.
Ils n'en trouvent pas à Plogoff, à Goulien, à Cleden, à Primelin.
Alors ils reviennent, ils les placardent, ils prennent une photo comme preuve, puis disparaissent.
Les affiches ne tiennent pas longtemps au mur.

L'occupation
Un hélicoptère effraie les oiseaux.
On l'appelle mère-poule.
Elle convoite ses précieux CRS.

La crêpe
Chacun a sa technique, mais la méthode la plus populaire
est de prendre une louchée de pâte à crêpe,
de la verser sur un bilig beurré, pour ensuite l'étaler en cercle avec un rozell.

La crêpe
Le moment venu, prenez votre spatule
et glissez-la sous la dentelle délicate
soulevant ainsi votre crêpe à la manière d'une traîne.

Déposez-la enfin soigneusement sur son autre côté, prête à recevoir.

La crêpe
Les premières fois que vous essayerez de faire une crêpe,
elle sera surement trouée et inégale, ou vous ne parviendrez pas à étaler la crêpe
assez rapidement, ce qui aura pour résultat une crêpe plus épaisse d'un côté, plus lente à cuire.

Dans les coulisses
C'est la veillée.

Le drapeau français en berne, le Gwenn-ha-du hissé.
Les dossiers de l'enquête brûlés par les quatre maires.
Une nuit blanche se profile alors que les ombres s'avancent,
les premières barricades se lèvent.

Our Lady of Tyres

We call our barricades the 5 o'clock mass,
and let me tell you, we've never been so fucking pious.
Our church is made of old cars and swearing,
our bones are tired but keep on giving.

Your Mother Hen, who hovers above us, may thunder fry her brains.
That's what we call your helicopter, that drunk wasp
who dives down on pensioners going to the market.
Her grenades come, her chicks have guns,
in our earth, as it is, your hell.

We fill your path with excrement.
We fill our boxes with piss and label them explosives,
sew diapers in the gardens for you to collect.
Give us this day our daily hail.
We fill your labs with our stormy discharges,
and Pollock your clothes with paint.

Our homes are an endless supply of horror.
Grandma's plates, the ones with the rabbit,
have been redecorated to look like landmines.
We send our kids out with colanders
on their heads, a wooden spoon in hand.
And forgive you your trespasses.

We live at the edge of the earth,
we've seen it at its worst, shedding
ships open like chestnuts, and you want
to fuck with it? Send us your worst
fungus-faced soldiers.
The sea always wins, child.

Notre Dame des Pneus

Nous appelons nos barricades la messe de 5 heures,
et je peux vous dire que nous n'avons jamais été aussi pieux.
Notre église est faite de carcasses de voitures et de vulgarités,
nos os sont usés mais ne s'arrêtent pas.

Votre Mère Poule, qui est aux cieux, que la foudre lui grille la cervelle.
C'est comme ça que l'on appelle votre hélicoptère, cette guêpe ivre
qui s'acharne sur les retraités se rendant au marché.
Que vos grenades viennent, ses poussins ont des 9mm,
sur notre terre comme dans votre enfer.

Nous couvrons votre chemin d'excréments.
Nous remplissons nos cartons de pisse et les marquons comme explosifs,
parsemons les jardins de couches usagées pour que vous les récupériez.
Donnez-nous aujourd'hui notre salut quotidien.
Nous remplissons vos labos de nos décharges orageuses,
et souillons vos vêtements de peinture à la manière d'un mauvais Pollock.

Nos foyers sont des réserves inépuisables d'horreur.
Les assiettes de grand-mère, celles avec le lapin,
ont été redécorées pour ressembler à des mines antipersonnelles.
Nous envoyons nos enfants avec des passoires
sur la tête, une cuillère en bois à la main.
Et vous pardonnons vos offenses.

Nous vivons au bord de la terre,
nous l'avons vue au plus mal, briser
les navires en deux comme des noix, et vous voulez
jouer avec ça ? Envoyez-nous vos plus redoutables
soldats au visage fongique et décomposé.
La mer gagne toujours, gamin.

Fox cull

In the bins of London are foxes,
hundreds of them, healthy and well-fed
on junk food.
Stalking through gardens
mauling babies
congregating together and attacking old women,
ripping the throats out of Vicars and Priests,
bombing the Houses of Parliament
and setting fire to the House of Lords.
Eating charity workers,
breaking into Buckingham Palace
setting up a guillotine
and beheading the royal family.
Climbing up Big Ben
and detonating themselves one by one,
sleek furry limbs flying everywhere
until all of London is on fire.

Julia Roberts

I was in bed with Julia Roberts, drinking wine at her Hollywood mansion in Notting Hill. She wore the slinkiest of garments and kept touching me. When I leaned in to kiss her, she froze for a couple of seconds then moved away, kept talking as though nothing had happened.

Soon she stood up, began putting on her dress and saying we had to go. We had to get ready or we'd be late for the party her Hollywood friends were having. Now it was my turn to freeze. She had not consented to that kiss. Was I another one of those creepy Hollywood men? Was I Harvey Weinstein?

'Are you ok? Are you coming?' she asked.

I said, 'Are we were alright?' Told her I was sorry for trying to kiss her if it's not what she wanted.

'Hey, it's OK. It's just I've never been with a woman before.'

'I'm not a woman.'

'You know what I mean.' I did. 'I love hanging out with you though, it's so boring spending all my time with those posh, rich people, you're much more fun.' I nodded.

After the party we lay in bed together in our underwear, drunk on expensive wine. Julia Roberts kept touching my arm and thigh but every time I moved towards her, she retreated, turning away from me to the glue and scissors and craft book laid out on the desk beside her bed. Easter crafts, she explained, and began cutting, but soon the cycle would begin again. She would touch me then retreat. After a while I gave up, lay back, and stared at the ceiling, eyes focussed on the tiniest speck of dirt her cleaner had missed. And I kept staring, even as Julia Roberts got up and silently left the room.

Anal

I want to bend over and take it like a man

A hole where my pleasure centre should be

Entered pleasurably only once, twice maybe

I know pain is part of the joy but always the tension, the hanging on

The client I told I wouldn't, maybe a finger or two, who said ok
and forced his whole fist in
and I didn't say stop exactly I said we'd have to stop *soon*
so it wasn't exactly   not that the police would
he had orange skin and played Vivaldi

The lover who liked to see me cry during sex
obsessed with entering   though we always had to end before we got going
she told me she enjoyed that brief
look of pain   exquisite moment of violation
as the silicon entered   I said I liked it too

That one Grindr guy was a revelation when we'd fucked enough
the other way   I opened and was hungry for it.
I remember the dark fur of his chest against my back,
how the weight of him made me relax.

The rubber-clad skinhead guy in the club
who fucked me raw   I'd never even heard of PrEP
kept asking him to come in me
truly a thrill
that drive towards

A hole that holds the body together

One time my therapist suggested I get to know my arse
so I smeared a butt plug with lube   amazed at the ease
with which the thing slipped   inside me
that night I dreamt of *Hollyoaks*, the episode where Luke gets raped,
in the dream it was Toby

Being Shadow

For my brother

On the off-chance that you might let me in,
I agree to sit compliantly at the head of your bed,
agree to have the dodgy controller, hope
to play our relationship on fast forward for a while.
Parkouring to an arcade soap opera theme, you batter
the buttons. I feel ringing in my ears. When my spin jump
doesn't make it, you turn
to look at me
for the first time

you're straight into rolling attack but
I am sat behind, remember? Your aura -
I would sacrifice everything. Maybe

we hit chaos control, suddenly you are
sat between my two kids showing them
how to spin jump, quick-step rivals.
They may be the wind, but
we are closer than you know.

Diary / Faces

Promises / Gappy toothy grin

I'm a princess. This dress swishes - pretend I'm dancing, there's no music. Sometimes I get hot and scratchy. I only half skip cos I know they're watching. They never dance. I stand still when they tell me, when they take my photo. They say I'm tall. I'm a good girl. I really want a dolly. I could talk to it and stop pulling my hair. They say if I'm good, the birthday fairies will come. I keep waiting. I promise to be -

Before (and after, if they could) / Resting bitch

Your skirt looks nice you say. You're really stunning, such long legs. My skin turns to chopped ham and cold custard. Their lips barely move upwards and if it wasn't for the clear throat and guttural tone, you'd think they were nervous. Hollow. I don't think they know that tights give you thrush. Don't you get cold? Don't your shoes rub? They wring their clasped hands as if feeling my pain already. Maybe pleading. Womanhood is risky: blisters or crusty cunts. Maybe frostbite. Have you had your hair done you say? Very dramatic. I wish I could be as brave.

What if? / Bags

Having shelled two healthy children – I'm lucky. Should I tell her that you only bake with fresh eggs? That you bite your lip, but don't always close your eyes? Will his father let him know? I keep this house as their incubator. Tonight, I will thank Jamie Oliver for the inspiration that produced another clean, colourful, med-inspired family meal that everyone will eat with enthusiasm. Without their warmth, there would be time for boredom. And thinking.

Nothing happened / Come to bed

A whore is a whore. (Un)dressed in the standard issue (ripped) fishnets and basque. Not even hiding behind those - Asking for it. Desperate. It is a satisfactory acceptance. A reason to be. You fuck the pain away. Afterwards, you shed that skin and develop new scales. Markings on the skin titillate. Their imprint. I imagine grass. Tall grass swaying sideways, like a slinky falling down stairs.

Role Play

I had on a couple of occasions indulged you in conversations about your art but today you were talking about your toil, your commute and the all-too-needy students who had been overly-mothered. They sit in your time like shiny pebbles damming the sea, you are the unwilling seaweed flung against their face. You think of them as the elves and you Father Christmas, but they are the kiddies desperate to sit on your lap and prove they've been good. Then you said it and I didn't know if I'd heard it, but you had. You wondered whether you had a case for pay discrimination, you were in the union. You thought it was a good sound case actually. Most men in your position with your experience get offered the senior post straight away and you wondered why you were stuck at the top of one scale, unable to make it over the stile. There was no helping hand to help heave you over and now you knew how it felt to be one of *those women*. Then you said, look at this video. I didn't know it would be you stroking your nipples. I realised then that you too were a kid sat on the lap of an older guy who is dressed up and muffling, pretending to know you and pretending to care. Was it more socially awkward to watch you tease your nipples to the sound of bad music or, to stand next to one another both heads turned down both muffling? Hoping to be the good kiddies. You didn't know how to audibly exhale through flared nostrils either. I looked at you then, sat in half hero, half lotus pose and I thought what a fragile little Barbie eunuch you are.

Bibliography:

Shadows of Burgundy (Penny Dender, 1965)

The Lark Sings Wind (Jenoimissyou Books, 1965)

She'll Have Her Way (Sylvia's Sweet Shop, 1966)

Blood Orchid (Dennie Swann, 1966)

Esther Perel, Listen To Your Heart (The Cypher Press, 1966)

Ripe (Danube Down Publications, 1967)

A Shakespeare Rítus (Hamisított Shakespeare-szövegek, 1967)

Library Lion Inside Out (Hyperion, 1967)

Diane Speaks of Derrida, The Human Abstract (Kaleidoscope, 1967)

The Fashion Dog (Literally Arts, 1968)

Seven Days in the Lark's November (Jane Cooper Editions, 1968)

Panorama Reiki (Danube Down Publications, 1969)

Appropriation des Idoles Résistantes (Charrue Presse, 1969)

Xenophobia Olympics Games (Szívesen Látott Bevándorlók, 1969)

Az Ellenálló Bálványok Kisajátítása (szántóprés, 1970)

Appropriation of the Resistant Idols	(Plough Press, 1970)
To This: Reportage On Revolutions, etc.	(A Touchstone Book, 1970)
Quilt	(Drum and book Club, 1971)
Think, Revolutions Everywhere	(Bell-nap Press, 1971)
Filling the Walls on Crinkleswell Road	(Humid Press, 1971)
North of Aries, South of Me	(Esplanade Books, 1972)
Radio Silence	(Kapcsolja be és ki újra, 1972)
A World in the Ocean, the Tower in Flames	(Stinging Nettle, 1972)
Centre of the Universe, the Mind in a Machine	(Hyper Atom, 1972)
Dialogue With a Visible Future	(Honesty Pubs, 1973)
Oraschin Tempa	(Daphniceleste, 1973)
Az Utcák Varázslók Nélkül	(Első szakasz Könyvek, 1973)
The Streets Without Magicians	(Knebel Verlag, 1973)
That Lark of Yours	(Collect Book, 1974)
Studies in the Vocabulary of Music	(Hyper Atom, 1974)
Words in Ink	(New Traditions, 1975)

Emerge	(International Tower of Poetry, 1975)
A Writ for the City	(Harmondsworth, 1976)
Time by This Time Tomorrow	(Bell-nap Press, 1976)
Thought Forms & Mistakes	(Intuit, 1977)
In Between Unbeing and Being	(Mary Lyons Publications, 1977)
Death Before Running	(A Slow Year, 1978)
You Used to Seem Lost To Us…	(Co-exit, 1979)
Poems, Material, & Other Notes on Ritual	(Jane Cooper Editions, 1979)
Vegetarianizmus	(A Stage Name, 1980)
A Plague of Doves	(A Postal Operation, 1980)
Sutras, Dawn's Head with Revelation	(Up-Holds, 1980)
On the Disappearance of Death	(All-A-Point, 1980)
Shod Maiden, Other Scenes	(First/Periodic Modern, 1981)
Magical Voices for Cthulhu	(Resplendent Voices, 1981
Of This Death I Pray Not and Father	(The Cypher Press, 1981)
Peculiar Souls	(Mid City Poetry Series, 1981)

June

Once and Future

Arthur C. Clarke, 1917-2008

That's him, crossing the night sky
above Manhattan, Sri Lanka, Borehamwood –
a UFO you might say, although

his own Third Law replies: *any*
sufficiently advanced technology
is indistinguishable from magic. The boy

from Bishops Lydeard (a Green Man puffs
his cheeks out in the church and Arthur sleeps
within the hill) held his breath beneath

home-made rockets, fireworks, until
he broke into the new millennium:
a sentinel, a spinning bone, a waltz.

*

We've lost our wise men, and are left with
the rich, who clamour like apes to be first
to climb the skies. We had dismissed it all

as science fiction until one day the moon
rocked our certainty, computers shrank
to the palm of a hand, and we held the world,

enthralled... which was when the virus wrote
its new version and the sea began to publish
our future. We cling on aboard a vessel

with no dialogue, only serious music
and a computer having a nervous breakdown.
He is safe, though, deep among the silver.

Newton

Gravity

He did not discover it,
he proved it
the tide
at Teddington Lock
recedes
They said
you are a magician
Isaac
the moon
over his mother's grave
at Colsterworth
draws closer
No,
he'll not deny
the sun
and respects
always the father's
absent authority

Optics

For two pounds a year
he has to be seen
to believe in the Trinity.

Time for a white lie
to be split into its
constituent parts.

A rainbow arches
from Lincolnshire
to the Mint.

Three Laws

That a fire in the laboratory
is never extinguished

That it is the error
unlocks the genius

That whoever pokes
a bodkin in their eye

sees best

Astronomer Royal

I observe the man –

he comes to the full
and his flaws show.

Sea of Unkindness.
Mount Arrogance.

In my star catalogue
his place is assured.

Ambitiosus.
Insidiosus.

But I am obliterated
from his universe.

Trinity Street

Outside the haunted house
crowds would hear
him as he passed: *meer*
cheats and impostures!

Back in his rooms, working,
he continued to ghost
any other scientist
who tried to get a look in.

Warden

The moon, uncounterfeited
as yet, saw how a dark glove

reached over to clip its edge
and scatter the silver, so

the stars came out. At Tyburn,
gravity claims another

coiner. At the Mint, Newton
has insisted on a raise.

King's Cross

The train at Platform One
is the 16.42
to Grantham

All about me
the world balances

The horse pulls against
the stone and the stone
pulls back

Epitaph

'...and All was *Light.*' My lightbulb starts to flicker.
His candle too. A message from the maker

to both of us that hiding at the back
there's something does not want to leave the dark?

After

'that is a fairy story for
people afraid of the dark'
— Stephen Hawking

The fairies fill the night sky:
the men at long telescopes
tell their story.

But they have no other light
to read by, so they have
overlooked the books,

the countless books
of glimmering moment
and sharp experiment

that might have shown
what they would never
accept as they count

on fairies and live out
in darkness dustily
ever after.

Fantasy Baseball Waiver Wire

There are two
counterspies on the edge
of the harbour and now
they see the boats
coming, the white
boats on the dark
waters of the harbour
and they move away
from the edge, they
are not looking, they
cannot face the boats

The sun is
rising slowly, the
tide is rising
slowly, the boats
come closer and the
boats come closer,
the sun is rising
slowly, the tide
is rising slowly

The counterspies
go on, they are
not looking, they
cannot face the boats,
the sun is rising
slowly, the tide
is rising slowly,
the boats come

closer and the boats
come closer, the
tide is rising slowly

The counterspies
go on, they are
not looking, they
cannot face the boats,
the sun is rising
slowly.

Beethoven's Thirteen Hundredth

I have a friend who cut her finger, and the flesh kept falling off. I have a friend who once shaved a cat in my bathroom and accidentally shaved the bathtub. I have a friend who once dropped a glass of water on a cobra and killed it. I have a friend who caught a water moccasin with his bare hands. I have a friend who ate a live shoe. I had a friend who swallowed a live scorpion. I had a friend who ate a plastic bag full of dirt and grass and she went into convulsions and died. I have a friend who drowned in a puddle of water and tried to find his way out by digging. I have a friend who touched his brother's mouth and he choked to death. I have a friend who drank paint thinner in a bathtub. I have a friend who got on a plane to nowhere to kill some people and then he was killed. I have a friend who tied a big stick to a pig's tail and it hit him in the nose and broke his nose. I have a friend who made a jellyfish sandwich and ate it. I have a friend who was a Navy Seal and he slept with the commandant of his course. I have a friend who hired a male prostitute who dressed in a spider monkey suit to drag him behind a truck. I have a friend who stole a pencil and wrote the word "LOVE" on a wall with it. I have a friend who got two peyote cactuses and ate them. I have a friend who stuffed dry leaves into her body and she went crazy. I have a friend who fell in love with a tree. I have a friend who cut off his own balls and made a necklace out of them. I have a friend who dressed in a bumble bee suit and tried to seduce a train. I have a friend who looked at her blood-drenched hand in the hospital and said, "Well, I guess I'm a murderer." I have a friend who studied the Swiss forest masters to improve her game of pool. I have a friend who mowed lawns for money. I have a friend who walked up to a convenience store and pushed a bag of dog shit through the cashier's window. I have a friend who told his teacher he was in love with the colour purple. I have a friend who sold postage stamps for a living. I have a friend who taught himself to sew and made a dress out of newspaper. I have a friend who sold pot. I have a friend who made a needlepoint of his face. I have a friend who told a doctor she was having sex with her own head. I have a friend who laughed when her boyfriend lost a goldfish in the toilet. I have a friend who sat down on a tiger's tail and stayed there until the tiger ran away. I have a friend who laughed when she cut herself shaving. I have a friend who put a black magic marker in his ear and it burned a hole in his head. I have a friend who chased a clown down a street. I have a friend who drank a whole bottle of Tylenol and swallowed a razor blade. I have a friend who went to the dentist for a cleaning and was shocked when he saw a baby tooth. I have a friend who ate a glass of water and fainted. I have a friend who threw a penny at a lightning bolt. I have a friend who swallowed a tree branch and broke his neck. I have a friend who swallowed a dead body. I have a friend who inhaled a balloon and passed out. I have a friend who urinated on an electric fence and got shot with a stun gun. I have a friend who ate a bottle of cologne. I have a friend who stuffed newspaper into his ears and then he got a headache. I have a friend who burned his nose and spat blood on a clown. I have a friend who wrote a brief article about himself in the newspaper. I have a friend who owned and managed a successful record store for 20 years. I have a friend who ran a newspaper. I have a friend who wrote a very good book. I have a friend who founded a small company. I have a friend who was stabbed in the neck with an ice pick. I have a friend who banged his head against a brick wall and was in a coma for two days. I have a friend who killed himself with a stapler. I have a friend who put toothpaste in his anus. I have a friend who performed oral sex on a banana. I have a friend who sewed his wife's hair to the waistband of his shorts. I have a friend who mixed his urine with alcohol and drank it. I have a friend who threw a pie at the Pope. I have a friend who set himself on fire in a mall. I have a friend who shit on the top of a moving train. I have a friend who put needles in his eye and didn't notice. I have a friend who used a shoehorn to put her head through a wall. I have a friend who put his head inside a grenade. I have a friend who chewed glass and his mouth and nose were sewn shut. I have a friend who put perfume in his ears and slept with one ear open. I have a friend who pinched his own nipples until they bled. I have a friend who wrote a bad review of the Toronto Symphony Orchestra. I have a friend who gave himself a bath and kept his finger in the water the whole time. I have a friend who bled to death from a paper cut. I have a friend who cut her tongue in half. I have a friend who bought $1.50 worth of gum and put $2.00 worth in her pocket. I have a friend who tried to eat his own hair. I have a friend who tied a knot in his shoelace and got blood poisoning. I have a friend who coughed up a lung. I have a friend who drowned in a fishbowl. I have a friend who sat in a bucket of fish. I have a friend who threw a jar of jam in a river. I have a friend who was swallowed by a whale. I have a friend who froze himself to death in a snowstorm. I have a friend who came out of the ocean with his skin on fire. I have a friend who shot a can off a roof to see if it would fly. I have a friend who had sex with a ghost. I have a friend who set himself on fire to see if he could feel it burn. I have a friend who set his car on fire and tried to crawl through the burning wreckage to safety. I have a friend who ate a cyanide capsule and survived. I have a friend who wanted to be an actor but got stuck in traffic. I have a friend who ate a package of nuts and was only served a second helping. I have a friend who climbed a fountain and drank the water. I have a friend who cut his ear off with a lawnmower and woke up the next day. I have a friend who dug his own grave and suffocated himself in it. I have a friend who built a catapult and wanted to know what it was like to be hit in the testicles by a shot from that catapult. I have a friend who ate a live moth and woke up two days later in a field of yellow daisies. I have a friend who took a pill and threw up in front of a mirror and got a great idea for a new sales strategy. I have a friend who shaved his face and chest in the same sitting. I have a friend who kicked a tree stump and made it explode. I have a friend who put a lit cigarette in her ear and blew it out with a shotgun. I have all these friends and not a single story to tell.

Oh God I've Peaked!!!

This plate
of nachos
was bought
for the sole

purpose of
eating the
whole fucking
thing. And not

one of you
could possibly
do anything
about it. This

fucking thing
I am eating
is going to
explode in

your goddamn
face. This plate
of nachos, it can
fucking suck

down everything
in the world
and *we love you*.
It would be

a fucking
crime if you
tried to eat
anything else.

Barn Owl

the moon is bright tonight
feathered ring of bronze
surrounding

cuts through darkness, thick, disturbs
no leaf, or strand of grass
unseen

sight is nothing, sounds cease mattering
but something surfaces where
nothing used to be

was it like the weight of occupied air
or conversation paused
solid?

the moon does not rest tonight
detaches raptorial
hover

from below they are fog curls, cloud cover
we cannot measure them
see instead

half-familiar faces
remembered from our dreams

Long Lane, near Felton Common

Spoon

It takes a while, but
he splits wood and strips away bark
from the pale interior

smells the oil
brings from the zip-pocket of his rucksack
a knife with a hooked end, whittles

moment by moment
the soft shape of a curved spoon.

The October sun is splintering
and all I hear is the *scrape scrape*
of blade

as embers from the fire hiss
he leans towards me, proud of his work

uses the thing he has made to scoop out
my eyes and eat them

leaving nothing behind

West Woods

Somewhere, Looking

on this beach night settles
there are black streaks on the sand

coat pockets clack with rocks
throwing stones and shells

around you wick things like candlewicks
reaching ends, their end of story
pale moths

you came here to occupy yourself
now search for driftwood, smoothed to bone

they do not expect to reach the moon
so burn, only knowing where to go
from before

this might have fallen in, you say
up the estuary, near breeding eels
and flown

clear when young, and like glass
see through, but seeing you

looking up, the moon paints the sea white
cratered, pinned moth to the sky

somewhere on the dark sand
something you dropped

the back of your neck aches
skeletally

you stoop low

SW 5780 4138

Middle School

When you love wrong your world ends
Phèdre Phèdre Phèdre Phèdre
Spotlight Telemachus detachment & singing

Ted Hughes gets to the end of his life
& writes that monster book on Shakespeare
The movie *Camp* (2003) is over a decade away

American teenagers doing musicals have not yet been
Apotheosized in Ryan Murphy's *Glee*
Nor has the spotlight's murderous intent fully

Revealed itself & so we have the poet reading
Desperately uncarefully
To feel something

New after translating *Phèdre* & keeping the grave
Accent on the title character's name
Among the only Frenchisms that survive

In a limpid but maybe-too-level free
Verse version the theater feels like the right
Place for Hughes to rip the heart out of his empty

Life à la Jonathan Pryce's character's threat
To Bond in that late '90s franchise entry
With the newspaper & the BMW

The threat will be carried out by another man
In keeping with the tragic tradition
But that is less important than the unity

Across all these myriad texts in how
They *lie* sometimes musically but always
In full view of a kind of truth

The viewer gets to hold most
Of the time or touch a little at least *see* it
Though once they do it reels them in brutally

To tragedy's machine
Old mug of Zippo lighters at the antique
Store the fire going out

In Phèdre's eyes jaundiced opposite of
Rachel Berry's Anna Kendrick's aqueous spotlit
Reflection round the iris on a held note

A thin annular structure
The jaillike perimeter of the American school
I'm about to go back to teach in one soon

& all this cowardly intertextuality is
To not deal with that fact
You know what's fucked is I did everything

I would normally do at the end of last year
But I didn't help my kids make their lit mag like
I had done the year before I forgot about it almost

Completely &/so it didn't happen
It's one of the only places in school kids can lie
Freely with no trouble (nobody reads it

But them) & then they can be the reader
For every piece other than their own & feel that glimpsing itch
Like writing will continue to haunt them

Until it has unknotted itself from the inside
Of their heart & lungs which doesn't happen to everyone
Like hey Ted got stuck doing it (or maybe was cursed to do it)

Through to the end

cw: trees

Two days after Jaden died
I posted a picture of a question
From the Arbor
Day Foundation Annual Survey

Do you ever relax
In the shade of a tree
Yes or No
Almost instantly

The pic got flagged
& taken down
Post removed for suicide or self-injury
I sighed, heavy, & continued

My long rehearsal
For a day without death

Minding the gap

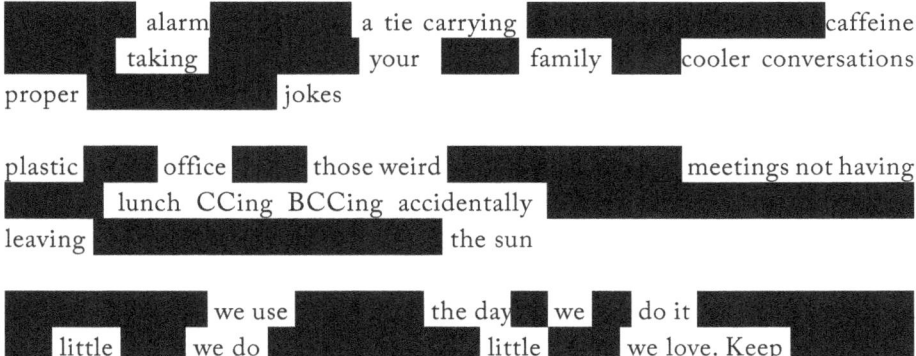

[redacted] alarm [redacted] a tie carrying [redacted] caffeine
[redacted] taking [redacted] your [redacted] family [redacted] cooler conversations
proper [redacted] jokes

plastic [redacted] office [redacted] those weird [redacted] meetings not having
[redacted] lunch CCing BCCing accidentally [redacted]
leaving [redacted] the sun

[redacted] we use [redacted] the day [redacted] we [redacted] do it [redacted]
[redacted] little [redacted] we do [redacted] little [redacted] we love. Keep [redacted]

Merge cells

stand under
head look down
gap between
breasts between
wall & spider
web scum
bubbles up to
knees fall scrape
scab webbing
digits loose
teeth weave
water up
to neck
Send & Receive
after weekend
or decay in
drafts paddle in
blood breathe
cutaneous
accept your
faith touch base with
the final merger

Outlook

The lever on the office chair deprives me
Of the feeling of whooshing down
Lowering myself into the weekend.

Pull violently. Nothing
happens. Perform desk assessment.
Take breaks by looking

At wall outside window.
Throw unnecessary items behind me.
Arrange keyboard in parallel with mouse pad.

☐Check clock
☐Dangle feet in water

Imagine
☐beer
☐a seagull
☐a chip

July

Joseph Stalin is Arrested at a Masquerade Ball by the Russian Secret Police, and Exiled to Siberia

(FEBRUARY 23, 1913)

I think that I shall never see
A pogrom lovely as a trial.

A triangle whose hungry murder is pressed
Against the winter's sweet flowing breath;

A trend that looks at godsons all deadbeat,
And ligaments of leafy armistices to pray;

A trespasser that may, in summons, wear
A neuter of romance in his haircut;

Upon whose boutique socialism has lain;
Who intimately lives with rampage.

Poetries are made by forfeits like me,
But only G-d can make a trial.

I: INTRODUCTION

An orchestral introduction before the curtain rises.

You whisper from the wings: "Plato called it a *daisy-world*,
Lifeforms self-evolving, the world
Is an eager mental health professional
Brought forth from chaos, as today's version of otherness.

Withdraw with me socially, me: a planet with
No thoughts to own but its own, several of sciences —
I just need a lot more time, I notice these changes in space,
I envision a perfect living system, a personal selection
According to help those in the daisy-world, show changes,
Separate the gods from time immemorial;
False opinions are fancy but more empathetic,
In ways most perfect, our universal fraternity
Questions new ones, severally,
This divine ploughshare cutting a life
That is so perfect, all in our other spirit worlds
And in ways that makes the personal central
And interconnected, malleable, unacceptable realities:
We are going to dance the earth out.
Not yet, but we are going to dance the earth out."

No he *didn't,* Vaslav. There are no interpersonal dimensions,
You just have unusual, over-valued thoughts.
More than anything else we should consult together
In the gatherings of psychosis,
And in the furrows of whimsy.
Though I'd love to withdraw with you,
You are far too delirious.
And sometimes you sound like a communist.
A swarm of spring pipes transcribed from ancient scrolls
Foretell that earthquakes are just wisdoms screaming to get out.

Ostinato

I care if you listen. The classics are ours. The basic line of music. Dialogues. Developments. Astonish me. Only art promises mortality. I'll wait for you to astound me. Madness is true of the normal heart. I'm severely afraid of dying in water. So many moments of happiness and anguish. I became nervous. I will eat everyone. I am man's firstborn. The murmurs endowed. Sit before the Alps, then picture the Himalayas. Do one thing. A common and sincere language: the Rite of Spring.

I'm there if you listen. The classical hours. The baseline of music. A dial-up envelopment. Astonish me. Only art promises morality. I'd hate for you to astound me. Madness is true of the formal heart. I'm severely ashamed of dyeing the water. So many moments of happiness in language. You'll become serviced. I will cheat everyone. I am man reborn in the fervour of crowds. I sit before the Alps, scripture the Himalayas. Do nothing. A common and austere language: the height of things.

Beware if you listen, the farcical hours. The hate crime of music, in spite of the strings. I care if you leaf through a catalogue. I'm there if you grieve a development. Admonish me. Lonely starts premise insanity. I'll wait for you to confound me. Gladness is true of a subnormal heart. I'm clearly ashamed of trying the water; so many moments of kidnapping language. Before our civil service I will cheat, hit and run. I am a dialogue, an excessive experiment. I am man stillborn. The brochure for shrouds. Sit before the Alps, write scripts for your players. Dialogues do nothing. Developments examine an unclear language: it's the hindsight that stings.

In prayer if you listen, the traffic is ours, it's the hate crime of losing to dialogues/developments in the light of all things, in prayer if you listen, I care if you listen with honesty in lonely hours; I'd miss the you of me. I'd hate for you to surround me. Sadness is you with a powder-horn heart. I'm nearly untamed when I'm close to the water, so many warnings from unwrapping language, before I do it disservice I tweet, hit and run. Fever is now. Be gripped unawares. Do something the night that we premier the playwright's new fling, a socialite sings a new prayer if you listen to dialogues. Beware if you hasten developments. Don't swear off a vision as dialogue. I care if you listen, repetitive stamping, no pattern of accent; the woodwind, percussion, the brass and the strings, just *sit down now.*

I care if you listen. Do one thing. A common and sincere language: The Rite of Spring.

Tulpa

A tulpa is an embodiment of such wish, desire, longing and/or love that it has become a sentient being in its own right — willed into existence by deep emotion, and no longer controllable by its creator(s).

And his name is Vaslav Nijinsky.
This genius would follow each person
From the hour of their birth
Until the moment of their death;
Smoky at the bedside like toothache,
Euphonic as laughter, but silent.

I know what you're thinking but a glow *can* be sharp,
And If you'd ever held an ammonite the sea hadn't got to,
You'd know that.
So I can say that the tulpa we made
Is radiance with teeth and a coke-nail.

Magnetars have unmannerly viciousness.
Breathing in is ridiculous and out is flamboyant.
My Vaslav is your Vaslav, what's mine is yours
So you are now the proud owner of a bouquet of clovers,
A flower but unsound, a mammal but fascinated
Because we fascinated him —
But let's give thanks to G-d that he's beautiful.

The rose-coloured gurgling can be heard in the valley,
Don't listen to who tells you it's a death-rattle, or grey,
And the pirouetting intellect inside that uproar
Will go mad. He'll go frighteningly mad.
And we'll have to watch him,
My hand in your hand.

This tulpa has become an infamy to me.
I have nestled in Vaslav's pockets,
Waited in Vaslav's wings and lived
In Vaslav's splintered landscapes, hipped
My shins to Vaslav's calves and put my
Hand over his mouth; we have loved his
Body between us, safer that way —
You don't know it, but you have a stake
In his grace.
I have read his diaries and held a pillow,

Vaslav's pillow, the Nijinsky grip,
"I am not crying but I have tears in my heart";
I think we are those tears, I think we
Therefore should be left alone
To gamble on the Stock Exchange,
Grieve, and do everything love commands us to.
Nijinsky hadn't the words to make the laws
For learning to wait in the air, he said:
"I merely leap and pause".
Healthy men rebuking their sick neighbours,
Vaslav moved into what we think
Might be our neighbourhood

And in our circling antiheroic undoings
Because sometimes that's what love is;
Fresh developments and influences from Moscow —
The Russian revolution: Limerence.
The eve of war: First night nerves.
The White Star Line: Go to the pharmacy?
The Rite of Spring: I love you.

It's often just enough to be with someone,
You don't need even need to touch them, or talk.
A feeling passes between you both —
You are not alone.

His name is Vaslav Nijinsky
And we let him come to the conclusion
That it's better to be silent than speak,
But then he danced appalling things
Far beyond our control.

And he thinks the earth will be like Mars
But in a few hundred years hence;
He has us looking for just one small universe
In which only secrets can survive.

Vaslav Nijinsky, my one big truth —
You are a work of art.
I'm sorry I got it as wrong as I did;

This *is* a fantasia.

<Ridgecrest, Best Western>

5am. A candle named PROTECTION lights the mirror darkness
of the street—

Springer to the South
Las Flores to the North
where last night
you chowed down
enchiladas verdes outside Olvera's.

[What did you do?

It was not enough]

Brother, in this light,
seeing / unseeing you

broken yet half-
recognisable

as
death
is.

The wick fizzes
grows dark—

Just close the door and go.

First thing you remember—

kicking in panels of glass
as mum and dad
warred
upstairs.

It was the day
he tried to strangle me.

It was the night
she came at me with a carving knife.

Brother, how to bury the sound of breaking glass?

[...]

If I could wash the blood from your feet.

The tears that
tear.

'R' *Ahhh*

—ROBIN—

'R' for 'Robbed'.

Ahh echoes night's chorus.

The 'in'
suffix

song - sheathed

echoing
out

(' ')

Everything
caught up with you—
the no,
the not yet.

Grief in the absence
of concrete nouns—

Sk(in)

(Ai)r

Br(other)

Death as contradictory gossip

. . . .

What was that?

. . . .

Sometimes I carry the portrait of your face
like carrying an empty wallet (′ ′)

All this. And this

[.................]

like trying
to assemble

the lineage of ashes.

SEA SILK

The last woman in the world who knows how to spin sea silk lives in Sardinia. Byssus mussels, four fish long, cling to the seabed by beard, secreted threads of silken saliva; 100 dives for 30 grams. Harvest it, preen it, soak it in a secret brew of spices — the result is so fine a pair of gloves can be folded up to fit into half a walnut shell. The woman sings into the spices: the cloth then illumes like gold. Plastic and Shell petrol are choking the mussels to death, these molluscs spoken of in the Bible, described by ancient Chinese wayfarers. Dive deep for the song of the ocean, says the woman. It cannot be bought, only gifted.

*

In Semporna, I've met Sama boys
who compression dive for pearls or
to fish-scare skipjack into nets —
they clamp their mouths over green garden hose
and dive down through a strata of blue on
dark blue, bubble-clad, sons and fathers and
uncles, the pressure on their skinny frames
so heavy they chance death.

Laughter over a cigarette.
A simple broth must do.

The hose, it glows, chugs diesel-tainted
breath from surface to poverty of light.
The bends swell joints to madness.

Their hair, it sways,
black as silt, as sable,
each fibre so delicate
it brushes the water
but leaves no mark.

They did not tell me if they heard any song.

MAHAKAM RIVER

The cadavers of giants are being lugged past —
legless, armless, decapitated — and on other barges,
piled up in pyramids, hard brown livers and burning
hearts in pieces, coughed up through chutes from the
killing field and haloed by their own dust — I lie on
the deck and watch them go by. Me, driven wild or
lethargic by longing, minute, minute, hour, diesel ghosts
and nasi kuning, fried fish heavy with heavy metals —
up from Samarinda, I am sailing, this journey so many
have made, brown highway connecting the tribes of the
interior to the Makassar Strait. At river's mouth crumble
stone teeth, traces of Kutai Martadipura, the oldest civilisation
in Indonesia, where the ojek boys rest on their bikes and fish
and flirt; I watch the swiftlets whir and flit, harden spit
for bird's nest soup, on a reverse *Heart of Darkness*.
Instead of a foolhardy European travelling into the centre,
fearing headhunters and cannibals, I am journeying to
the interior of me. Local myths say you go upriver to the
land of the dead, but right now, it feels like life reborn. Softly
I hover the eddies — dark silt bed might make good grave.
Wayfarer in the homeland — I could never think of Ireland
that way, though that is the other half. The locals think I am
Arab until they hear me speak Bahasa, poorly, and ask for
pictures of my family — ya, kamu orang Dayak — then sell
me embroideries and tell me it is election season. They say
the capital of Indonesia is soon going to be moved here.
Jakarta is sinking into the sea.
I reach a point where I can go no further,
but not the source — never, it seems, the source.

Mr Muhammad holds up the skull of a leopard; he shot it
in the jungle. There are human skulls in the roof of the
longhouse — 'we don't take heads anymore. Well, it's okay
if someone's really bad' — stories carved in the
beams, boars and buttocks, things I will never understand.
The men are re-skinning a drum, smoking, wrapping
it tightly into place with sinew, testing it for resonance,
calling in a storm that beats its own rhythm, on the streets and
river, falling syllables, like 99 names of God, repeated,
and all the spirit names of animal and ancestor.

My skin, silver with rain — touch it with the tuning fork.
I promise, it echoes too

I cried again in the night, sought

the little dent on the left side of your forehead,
running fingers across
thick bristle brows that hood your eyes,
a brown scape haloed with gold,
irises framed with the window's

light
touches your hair, a soft mass of black
spreading, your limbs run over mine.

Deep set in the bed
you rock me,
and your smile, felt through tears –
a warmth I cannot contain.

The morning – it comes and you stand above,
a vignette of muddled longing and hope.

Today is a Rothko painting,

blue rectangle over a warm
cream one,
yesterday's heat now softer.

Today is a chapel, light
singing through windows,
whispered colours
coalescing

outside, the sun-bleached
sky at midday.
Inside, today is linen -
stretched, soothing.

Another to cross.

Through a solar panel sea outside Retford,
the train is a ship speeding through waves
and it becomes hazy
watching one landscape fall to another,
fishermen thronging
along the banks of the River Trent.

They catch shoals, I catch breath,
and we've collected pronouns and accents
stretching the course of this country,
and I have aged.
Another hour another minute
another, wait, a second
a brief respite,
before the ticket collector comes to check my railcard
and I see my face three years earlier,
that version close to expiry.

Next September I will carry a quarter of a century
in a new city, new haircut, new purpose
and I'm fearful of losing friends. Lovers. Time.
Now into Kings Cross, the tube.
Another line to cross, one more platform falling away.

Alexandria-Crete-Aden *1880*

In Alexandria, there was no work.
Set sail for Cyprus. Bullshit, but not to worry,
I'm hard-but-fair, the foreman in a quarry.
I keep an eye, make sure they graft, don't shirk.
Course, there's always one who tries it on.
Don't take that bad-mouth back-chat. Should I be sorry
I threw the rock that cracked that bastard's head?
He fell. Sparked out. His gang was mean, but stunned.
I left him there stone-cold. Not *for*, but really dead.
Don't hang about. Too fast for getting caught,
I'm gone. What could I do, but get the fuck
double-quick down to Limassol, the port?
Got rowed out to a leaving ship. Pot-luck.
End up in Aden, hinge of Empires, stuck.

*

Dark Continent by cart, horse, camel, dhow.
– I'll be absolutely modern now:

a practical, read-the-market sort of Seer.
– Could raise a son to be an engineer.

A Man of Science, with instruments and charts.
– I'll trade: sell coffee, ivory, mechanical parts.

Time to hunt down that real but absent Life.
– Have money. Power. Servants. A dark-skinned wife.

I watch the caravans, all fully-laden,
arrive and leave where East meets West in Aden.

There's opportunity here. I'll make the most.
– Just got a job at Bardey's trading post.

Head Office

Aden, again, January 1883

I saw the future: could be the coming man.
Somehow it hasn't quite worked out to plan.

I'd been there a year, and though often ill,
had got to learn the trade and oiled the wheels,

explored the territory towards the Ogaden;
had plans for other expeditions when

Bardey called me back to head office here.
Now, it's already another wasted year

of kicking my heels, stuck in Aden again.
I plot and plan. Like mice. Like other men.
I ask myself: *And if not now, then when?*

Last Rites

A priest's been summoned by Isabelle,
with all the sacred impedimenta.
He hovers to hold me back from Hell.
Been there before. Am I slipping back,
spiralling down to the Dantean centre?
Once did that trek, since covered my tracks.

What good is this? These Rites, my last?
Forget Communion, or Confession.
Forgive me, Father: no intercession!
Not even God can change the past.

This life is pain, disappointment, grief.
This priest, peddling Salvation, God,
requires the suspension of Disbelief.
I'm earth to earth, just sod to sod.
O, ever since the damned Year Dot,
we've all gone from life, its strange mishaps,
like Voltaire, towards a great Perhaps... or Not.

I am the poet's sister Isabelle:
my brother has been spared from Hell!
Arthur surprised us with his piety.
He died in Christ and will live forever! PRAISE BE!

An Selected Poems

If I was a submarine I'd wish I could fly.
These spoons are no good
but porous and dissolve in my tea.
You look confused.
Why don't you get out the kitchen
(my kitchen is outside).
And while we're on the subject, how many of ye here can say
I too am the spinach delving rod.
Don't throw up unless nonetheless wiser sideways goes drop
in the town of my enormous fluorescent upbringing
an ice-cap breaks free to fuck off.

Chunk Identification

The life not lived sentimentally
justifies the one lived. Pulled by
ideas outside the close captioned frame
the lag equates the quality
and quantity of human life.
Even now the ghost
takes shape in the model of linguistic refraction
in which one thing
is mistaken for another – concise
and extractable like a modular component
or this or that universal socket,
where every distinction is but a fine point
on the physiological preconditions
of what we call reading the page,
the fine point infinitely small
shuddering in the branching clades.

This is Not Just an Elegy for a Schoolmate

Stumbling down a main road
a death-threat inside an Ebeneezer
Howard or Geraldus Cambrensis
effluent, cashed out to the middle-classes
to avert the ills of socialism, all that
dribbled into your dead ear by a parish epidermis.

People's experiences are different, but not that different from
a cat in tenth-century Wales.
To determine its value its head was held down

its tail was held up and grain was poured over it
until its tail was hidden, and the cat
was worth that much grain. Stop hitting

yourself like the dopplering
of a field or a painted horse, I remember barely speaking to anyone
and you screaming in French on cue always. 25 grains.

People either pull a whitey or have at it, so many
casts hide evidence of something that might
be self-harm but why talk about it.

I remember my sudden death after a fight
with my father and dying
in a tunnel under a supernova and knifed for a
cigarette at the Carrigaline roundabout,
a kind of disgusting gelatin

buildup nearby in scaffolding, quivering and/or
glistening, choose your own adventure,
the whole thing not helped
by that frog discovered skewered on the beak of
Barry Collins, which was at least a better option than what.
Broken arguments trundle on. Minds are wrecked then not,

get wrecked or not or the grotto bursts into
a shimmering five-dimensional
barbed-wire, forming the text of whatever band

any number of people could have made it in. *Homeromastix.*
None of your experiences are yours anymore.
Counterfactuals stupefy, the wrecked is harder or the absence
of care for each other or giving into let's jump off that roof
      but never get skilled at it. 15 grains.
Balls caught on the gutter and all.
   I don't want to catch you I want to laugh at pain.

When I go back to where I come from and it is not Christmas
        no-one is there, all emigrated – those with degrees,
                    largely to London,
                       those with none to Australia or New Zealand

/ A recoil pours sauce on the sun. Standing with a tenner
in the interior of three regicides (which wouldn't be enough),
cruel laughs vent minute pandas into actions
         on another's behalf

drowning in grain then an inverted topography just to go halves on
      a nodge, which isn't at all like how everything baby animals do
is a further exaggeration of what is already happening. It's 30 grains
now, but the fifth attempt.
Are we the ground or the accountant? The cat was just one
      of many vague predicates in a moshpit, welcome

     inside the pearly gates of C. Harvey Rorke, 'An early
pricing model regarding the value of a cat:
A historical note,' *Accounting, Organizations*
   and Society 7.3 (1982), pp. 305-306.

Shame is our social relation. How could you have been
so still, in the growing pile.
   To be honest, I imagine it is already like
  no-one ever *really* knew you.

I'm a monster. Passion is for lice. Sentiment is a knife.
Sentiment is poppers
   round the carpark. Just strike the counter, growl again
and snap the band round the throat in something
which maybe is maybe isn't IS IT YET a heap.

i.m. Paul Hodder

August

Buried Boys Always Come Back

The buried boy beneath my heels
returns with a scalpel
How is he complete, *Achilles*?

When unable to talk about
anything but ligaments
The fibula, the calcaneus

And his mouth full of leaves
Maybe figments left over
All fallen off

Or purposefully pushed in
To the top and bottom of the frenum
Ankles cut at forty-five degrees

Voice like October he appears
Can't talk about Ouija, *bad luck*
or the current consequences of

For those with cracked fingers
Trodden on and bruised, at the nail-
bed, at our knuckles

Man Considers Climbing Out Of His Body & Into Another

Though when we do this,
will they come for me?

Their claws, their quick hands.
A breathing in and out of walls.
To the land, a sowing of seeds.

My truth is
buried beneath the floor.

They fill the quiet places,
between pillows and sleep.
When a door clicks in the night.
When a child holds a finger gently
like a twig.

This lull behind my face,
This gap.
This lingering between.

They will knock you with a Gavel.
Ring the hood of your skull as the
upward fields grow green,
and the tree -

The tree outside is leaning in?
To listen?

To listen, feel.
To wrap roots around a
house heaving up its
skirt of earth to run away.
Dust in an attic space.
The spill of dreams through
gaps in a worn sash.
In sleep, hurt skin holds
the sound of trains.

(Gather pace then, tentative heart)

How would they come for me?
Pain in lieu of love?
Deep water to drown?

Deep and yes

How high will the crops grow?
How hard will it be to
harvest them?

Very tall.

Very hard to.

But I'm little and
afraid to fall.

Present beneath everything,
below it all.
A talk of thinness.
Of exhalations blowing
down bricks.

Little pig   *Little pig*

Please

Let me climb in

Wolves at Distance

Voices in the oak trees, the dribbling brook.
Widening arms a wingspan. A vice holding
onto limp bodies drawn upwards by the
masseter, the pterygoids.

The crown of that church lipped as a tabletop.
Two scattered barrels shortened by a blade
and the memories of a sister stooped lonely on
its grounds beneath a fractured steeple, a roof.

A cranefly muted by a nearby howl. Its fragile
leg twitched on a palm and whispers tumbling
through the ryegrass. The hollowness a sphere
brushed against a gradual skin.

Roughened sisal rope burning though the
crease. Weeping bark notched; pitch sticky.
Of all the swinging weight. Botched daylight
bares sickle teeth, O slow yellow crescent.

The Kill

The river where the man made us untuck our shirts is fenced off and full of trash. Beneath my legs, right angled, the phalanx is cramping. White roses are torn up and scentless in a heap. I've been to Europe, Beijing, Los Angeles. Ungrateful of me to think that there are more beautiful places. A more beautiful body to live in, more meaningful work. Not just numbers, not *just* the numbers, or some mad caricature blowing breath into jars for comparison. Because a career is the lack of depth felt between sunrise to sundown. So let me reward you then, with dialogue. The words made by old mouths for the new and obligated. As a forkful of the rarest meat, the *manliness* of a tomahawk steak. On how to hunt, to drown out feeling. Be a sinking stone arcing downwards to an open palm, an awful finger. I wish that I could tell you my name or who I am. That I'm stretched out. An old button accordion, a trophy kill.

At the school for assassins

they had us
studying piano drop montages
for hours at a time: every gram
of their bodies aching to return
to ground level, the pulley
snap, the flattened passersby
or phew-that-was-closes.
An upright emits a wooden
gasp, then bassy resonance
dampens to hum to
meet the tone of our breaths.
Better students moved on
to sharper concerns, the finer points
of dagger upkeep, the eight
fatal strike points. We stayed
in the projection room past nightfall,
permanent imprints
in the beanbags, falling
behind. We left
with no diploma, but can judge
if a baby grand wants tuning by the timbre
as it smashes into asphalt.

At a party full of old classmates,
now contract killers of note, us dropouts
insisted on an icebreaker game
of wink murder. Your body
percussion on the floor,
a painterly pose, with Buckfast
pooling where you let it fall.
I hijacked the playlist, swapping
Tom Petty for industrial techno
and after that is blackness.

The last time we talked,
I'd let the few miles
between us elongate. We hid
from tipsy acquaintances on the balcony.
The moon appeared as a bright pebble
dropped into a well, to check for the splash
that proves nothing's bottomless.

Before I left, to pedal back
along a clear canal path
you held me long and hard.
When Alex called, weeks later,

the room went monochrome. Sounds
muffled, as if through felt.
My voice dropped
to a creaking register.
I never learnt
which bridge exactly.
Whenever I cycle
beneath one, there's this jolt
and I get off to push, a
stiff half-step then its echo,
till my blood stops buzzing.

When a human falls like that,
a piece breaks off the world,
like with each heavy rain
this rented house gets
thinner.
You never expected

me present at the railing
or as crumple zone below
to cushion the thud.
I apologise often regardless

to your digital shadow,
for falling back. My messages
remain unread, stack higher
like scaffolding braced against the wind:
A video of a cat you would've liked,
that stupid song was playing in the taxi,
I found a baggy two-thirds white
on the floor of the cubicle
and pictured you behind the stall divider
saying, *Don't think about it.*
And it's good to hear
your voice and feel that familiar
weight in my hand.

The Agency

I ate the mushroom
growing on the wall of the downstairs toilet
in the house we rent. I folded
a thick slice of brown bread around it
and gobbled the lot raw. They might try
charging us extra at the end of our tenancy
because the mushroom wasn't meant for us.
But in their assessment, what is? See
what I have in my hands. It's nothing.

See it moving. Like devotees
bowing round a colourful altar.
They forbid us painting over the white
but I painted anyway on the white
of the sink with the rainbow
of my vomit. I am

thirteen again. I am hovering
a foot above the ground like a god. They don't want us
skating on their office block steps as if
the concrete isn't there for us. Smooth
as a dream of endless falling. Shouting
watchmen emerging to shoo us off the premises.
What are they thinking,
that they can contain this? It's only
my folded arms holding me together.
If I raise my hands towards the sky,
so bright and boundless I ache,
a thousand canaries will take flight.

After the Attack

The campsite was still standing.
You produced that battered set
of travel chess, as if nothing had happened.
As if all in the vicinity hadn't listened
to final confessions of my every fuck up.
A speck of air-light ash settled in my trouser cuff
but it was only Roz frying vegetarian sausages.
She was singing some upbeat pop hook.
It didn't make sense, my persisting.
The forest shook,
didn't it? The psychopomps collared me,
didn't they? Skidding into sight
in flashing vans. Yet, here was the sun's refutation
on the valley, grass become solid underfoot, the blood
only a few blotted drops
where brambles had snagged on skin.
Come on, you said, *it's your move.*

The stars in Florida

are like cystic acne
so many of them
and just as human
blinking in
and out

A part of me

does worry that neither of us will ever be able to leave this place.
It's some time now that I've been living in your head, quite on your benevolence
or perhaps the indolent procrastination of a somewhat kinder landlord
than others.
Strangely, you don't seem to mind that I make of you my medicine cabinet,
that I tear down the walls around here and put up kitschy wallpaper.
In order to get with the times, I've had a sex change from nymphet to CCTV
and, in my spare time, am your eyes.
To escape the impossibility of our perfection,
a dog that I baptized "loneliness in two"
(or maybe just the sadness of the past, which, I was surprised to find, carries on even when you are "very much in love"),
I spend my days painting frescos on the wall:
"angels playing music", already faded. When it grows dark,
I take the nail supplements poorly and put on my Disney princess dress, the itchy one, sit down with my hands in my lap,
and wait for the room to tremble as you begin to speak.

Personal apocalypse

I feign tiredness, I rub my eyes,
to hide the pity in those weary globes.
It is possible that Cain was unable to find his words,
that, just like his father, he stuttered before the block of his Father's brow.
I call it a glimmer of goodwill, that hesitation among the rubble.

How many times should I betray you
before your pride gives up the ghost?
There is supreme comfort
in the fatso lace doily topped armchair of self-betrayal.
You're a bracelet bought in Venice on holiday and lost at school,
a choochoo train,
a Tamagotchi that I locked in a desk drawer.
You are who you no longer are.

If God were in the room with us,
I'd ask him to cover my eyes with his hand,
like fever, like bedtime, like burial mound,
although when it comes down to it,
anxiety is like interventional radiology.

Look at me.
I'm prematurely old, like a rotten piece of cake,
and that paunchy American harvest moon that we are both under, dead or alive,
is the luminous and happy yellow
of first date French fries.

Working Titles for this Poem Include...

brown school skirt in honour of those stiff and unforgiving pleats.
How they buckle and warp when the waistband
is rolled.
You walk from school, through town, past the prison, home,
imagining what life will be like
when you are older.

C*astles for Cosette* and *Tunnels for Eponine*,
distant gunfire over a papier mâché
motte-and-bailey castle you made at junior school.
It is a skill to build defenses against scalding oil cauldrons and quicklime;
to mould cotton-wool sheep and pipe cleaner battering rams.

A castle is a room in which to hoard
ambitions,
where you pack relics into tea chests, along with expectations.
Later, you yearn for *lost sketches* of moon faces
and tiny triangle bodies,
of that house you loved, a box with a chimney,
an accident of birth in felt-tips.

M*uch too soon* for the Greek waiter you met in Rhodes at fifteen.
Far too old for the DJ who pushed your head
into his lap in a lane.

It is your *part-time job* at the Stakis, and a scum-filled bucket of cutlery to polish
at the bronze package hotel where dreams discolour and tarnish.

Cycling at speed, anorak flapping,
gum wound around your tongue, standing
outside Benetton at eleven in your knee-
high boots,
with your *childhood like a siren* screaming *wait!*
Not so fast,
as you lean against the milkshake splattered telephone booth.

No, you don't worry about time or loss on that walk home from school,
that today might be *the last day your mum*
picks out your clothes.
So confident you'll never want for more or leave.
Your *idyllic, painful, naïve teenage years*.

Submerge

She contemplates a mourning sea,
set alight with algae, sprinkled with smooth,
broad swimmers' shoulders.
Rhythmic treading, chestnut bodies four feet
from the beach gauge the day's impending
toil and heat.
In front, a line of *medusae* guard the shingle strip
take watery sentry posts at daybreak,
link tentacles to form a wave attenuating fence.
She glides past those who have not missed
this daily ritual in seventy summers
and with fresh welts turns to survey
the shore. Unlike a jellyfish, she has a brain
but doubts her instinct for survival
swoop siren, dive under.
She is touched by mysterious creatures, half-a-billion
years old, her neat square of belongings,
a tear on the rocks,
as she joins the choral bobbing.
With skin salt-crisped, hair in ropes
a spark of gelatinous energy jolts her from reverie.
She returns to the sand, examines the keloid fan-lashes,
smokes cigarettes on worn, striped chairs
swim now, fix later
goes back to primitive fantasies of breaking
barriers, of changing the tide.
The livid purple scars stay for a week, then fade.
Cells absorbed. She never swims in a dawn ocean again.

The Lament of a Future Daughter of Neptune

A day away from slimy induction
by the King and his helper.

Across the Equator's watery line,
they catch a fish.

We stand transfixed as the silver light
swoops and sways on its cord
through the waves.

Then — hoisted and hooked,
bashed and sliced, blood sprayed
into scuppers,

all remains cleaned
from sun-bleached decks —
they hold her up.

We smile, recoil.
Peer into one unblinking eye.
Register nothing.

Just a baby, they say,
as they gather their tools
and begin their work.

Mermaid Visits the Archive

After Adrienne Rich

By the shore, she recalls
once diving the wreck.

Though they told her never
to adventure its depths

or harvest its bones, cast
as oracle on ocean floor.

She witnessed a rotten hull
give way, from tarry gloom

the dull gleam of mercury,
copper ingots' cold clink.

She longs to recall the stink
of death. No documents

but papered dissolution.
She seeks herself in ivory

and iron, salt-cured skins,
elephant tusks, stone shot,

fragments of pelvis. Later
she learns to hide her tail

beneath long skirts. Land–
dweller, she gathers a form

from museum dust. Between
mammoth & meteorite, she

reads of affinity with elephants,
her twin pairs of breasts–how

when strapped to a mast, she
gains ecstasies–a voice pitched

to scream, which some sailors
call her song. She feels the stones

weighting her chest. Ghosts of
coins spill silver from her mouth.

Dreaming Blue

You close your eyes to an oneiric hum of darkness.
Feel the water's insistence, how calm latency stirs.

Symbols arise, slow birthed from refractive deep.
Minor tentacled creatures surface, writhe amid

a milk froth of waves. Always alone in dreams, you
comb littorals on broken mnemonic shorelines.

Saltwater corrodes silence. When you speak in old,
eroded tongues, it's too late. The sea will not sing its

ancient history, nor jettison epiphany to you: struck
mute, no song worth sharing. Refusals are wracked at

your mouth's open cave. Wiping grit from your eyes,
you watch whales on the remote horizon, sounding in

monumental curved skulls. Imagine blue-skinned Vishnu,
adrift on Ananta, the serpent. When the world becomes

hopelessly oceanic and playful, Vishnu begins to dream
of a golden lotus seeding his navel. How on its blooming

a cosmos scatters. Once more, the universe spins.

Trilogy

I

Opening shot. *Girl* on a battlefield. The camera pans numberless dead. Round black mouths slack open, defeated fish gulp a copper-tinged sky. They lie cadaverous, shaven-headed, eye-patched, skin-sutured. Close-up, *Girl* is unblemished: hair pure & whip-like or chestnut & tumbling. Pale eyes of steel grey or verdigris. Her armour welded from hubcaps & tyre, tailored skin-tight, hip-hugged by slick holsters. Slung upon her lithe spine a quiver of arrows. Arching her back, she squints, takes aim like Gramma showed her. Gramma died of the end times like everyone *Girl* loved. *Girl* is alone now. Two actors vie for her affections: one a music star the other an influencer, to represent old & newly dystopian worlds.

II

Girl embodies apocalyptic renewal: cityscape of exhausted rubble, farms burned stubble. Techne mere fire, spit & old wire powered by batteries from innards of infernal machines. See *Girl* parkour cyborg precision over rusted hills, burnished gold sky, mercurised river. Embittered, embattled *Girl* meets her rival's gaze down a gun barrel. Weeps only when she loses the bronze talisman about her neck. A dragonfly wing? (No. It is literally a seed pod.)

III

So many years of her life pass for six hours of film. At trilogy's fin, *Girl* walks lone charnel ground. Dodges bullet rain, seeps fake blood to fill a river. She's tired of the influencer, whom she wants to kill. The music star is secretly married. Ending a wintertime of spare & barren, we are reminded *Girl* will flourish. *Girl* will blossom in spring, bear fruit at fall. Epilogue of fields tinted saffron. Grass, wildflower, corn & hayseed. Settler recuperation. A land left unclaimed (like a woman) is no nation. *Girl* in floral frock holds baby: cute assembly of violence & desire, celebrity & guilt without reparation. **Fadeout.**

pete davidson (ariana grande could never)

recently i've been daydreaming of pete davidson

this is not unordinary   they come to me like woodlouse

crawling out of piles of damp leaves onto the knees of late school children

my daydreams are not jabberwockys caning cans of red bull, much simpler, instead

on one hour walks i look at wooden tables leaning against closed pubs think *hmmm*

if i happened to run into pete davidson on this street corner would we

fall in love with a badly delivered joke over a glass of soda and lime?

would we sit outside, oblivious to onlookers scouring my hands for seven rings?

how long would it take for opportunists with cameras to get lucky?   i can see it

my head turned in slight shock, he, a library statue, all knowledge

in my newest fantasy i am wearing sunglasses that don't hide my face

and he is pale, so pale the sun decides to shine on him directly like a detective's desk lamp

        'what do you do in the shadows?' it asks

i tell the sun to soften on his features and offer him factor 50

he is grateful i am the good cop

later, i walk along brighton beach, lick my lips between waves retching on the shoreline

and play this image in my head over and over again

my feet the mechanism transforming my eyelids into a private cinema

audio playing 'this is okay' with too much fervour to be wholesome

when i go home i hesitate to write this down

what if one day he sees this poem?

my woodlouse fantasies, childish and toxic like a chalkboard his ex wrote the song 'pete davidson' in the whirlpool of their relationship

now she is married to someone else i can't help but hope he is not clinging to the side of his life
  wishing for armbands

pete, i whisper to the other side of the dark *don't drown*

i will be your lifeguard

and halfway across the world on the light side of the moon

he drifts off and i sing

pete davidson and i meet in a crowded bar

we are in manchester because i know he has been here before

and my daydreams are nothing if not attentive to the details of realism

i am working on a poem, which is for once
not about him

and he asks me about it

so i describe to him how the universe can be kaleidoscopic and monochrome all at once and he laughs

in a subtle way to let me know he understands

a hand reaching for your finger in a room where the lights go out suddenly and you need to know at least one person won't murder you

my hair is in a ponytail and we make small talk on the type of high stools no one really wants to sit at

our backs curving to gravity and the weight of my expectation

i drink whiskey and he doesn't, because in my daydreams i believe him

and we leave the bar together

deciding where and how far to go

pete davidson and i get married

cue the church bells and the white dress

cue the tabloids printing every headline

cue the bets on how long it will last

i couldn't care less, i am wearing silk in spain

and my husband kisses me like i am oxygen as we cut a cake

made out of glitter and carnations because fuck it why not

sugar is a plastic fish nailed to the wall

only love could touch every part of the tongue on this day

delicate and dackering in the neo liberalism of our union

yellow dressed dappled light, sparkling water fountain suits

sit on tongues like bees resting on a flower

phoebe bridgers and tom misch play the first song

and they cover harvest moon so beautifully

silk chiffon teeth, eyes like forest fires

there is not a dry eye in the house

i wake with a wet face

September

On Hermann Hesse's Narcissus and Goldmund, *1930*

circles and we don't even know that we are going around in

Because the Sky Is Lighter Than Paper, a Manifesto of Feathers

I.

blue because my wings are the bookman's pages

blue because the island is holy, the wind high

blue as in azure as in cadmium as in noise

blue and black because kisses hurt

blue when they saw me, they saw us

blue the night we were walking home, josh, you and i, and the thugs

blue the night outside the art gallery when they chased us, unwing'd

II.

blue like mary's robes

blue like the altar boy gown i wanted because it was fabulous

blue when they threw me out the church, and i dreamt of jesus truly

blue and the cherub has turned

blue and the angel has turned

blue into blue into krishna

blue and i saw him one day in my dreams

blue shirt of blue school uniform

blue invisibility

blue, he touched my spine and flutes sang in me

blue, both mirror and mute

III.

blue the walls, the stones, the tomb

blue once, but now *coolitude*, *créolité* blue

blue *indienocéanisme,*

blue *antillanité, négritude, batiment* not batty man

blue for the way my heroes are dying but

blue mad for the second coming

blue veins on every dick i ever sucked

blue power, blue notes, the currency of

blue, melodies, you, rubber orchestras, true

blue blood & blue-collar &

blue scrubs fighting red coats

blue ink for blue manifestos of

blue feathers, disobedient walls, graffiti is

blue, jab molassie is

blue, and maybe—

the second coming

Super Blue Blood Moon Valentine

it was full moon but not an ordinary full moon and somehow the night was blacker than usual and that just made the moon's light so much more magnetic and the sea was churning and really it was like watching silver leaf being crumpled and he had this act where he pulled out a glass ball and I was astounded because of the rum punch yet there was some degree of uncertainty as to how I was going to get home but the Midnight Robber told me there was a gay fete going on across the street and I think he wanted me to come with him and I wanted him but I didn't know if tonight I could feel safe I never feel safe I wanted to swim and feel safe like the time I went skinny dipping with my cousins and I think that was how they told me they loved me

On Salvador Dalí's Metamorphosis of Narcissus, *1937*

Looking, your metaphors crack open
Looking, your metaphors crack open
Until flowers bloom and stones are dogs
Until flowers bloom and stones are dogs
Your metaphors crack open, until
Flowers bloom and stones are dogs

Someone praying, a sprinter at a starting line, a hand, an egg
Someone praying, a sprinter at a starting line, a hand, an egg
How the fingers hold the testicle
How the fingers hold the miracle
A sprinter at a starting line, a hand, an egg, how
the fingers hold the testicle

The flowers are dying
The flowers are dying
Ash clouds
Ash clouds
Flowers are dying, ash
clouds

Until ash clouds bloom and stones are flowers
the praying will be forever dying – a miracle how metaphors crack
open at someone starting a lie, a sprinter, a hand, the testicle,
an egg the fingers hold,
your dogs,
looking

TEST PATTERN (OLFACTORY BOYHOOD)

1. Pine Tree
2. Ovaltine
3. WD-40
4. Rhubarb
5. White-Out
6. Ammonia
7. Dirty Band-Aid
8. Saliva
9. Yellow Pages
10. Dried Semen
11. 80s Wood Paneling
12. Bicycle Tire
13. Angel's Trumpet
14. Jockstrap
15. Sex Wax
16. Werther's Original
17. Gasoline
18. Pork Sausage
19. Dunhill Red
20. Legos
21. Hustler Magazine
22. Rust
23. Talcum Powder
24. Skateboard
25. Smegma
26. Red Spray Paint
27. Arancini
28. Nivea Hand Cream
29. Taxidermic Moth
30. Leather Racing Gloves
31. Opium by Yves Saint Laurent
32. Cheesecloth

33. Grass-Stained Denim
34. Shoe Polish
35. His Hands
36. Diesel
37. Gangrene
38. Pernod
39. Elmer's School Glue
40. Black Mold
41. Football
42. Steel Butt Plug
43. Chloroform

LATE DECEMBER

Clearly. Nothing much is happening. Kids continue to wish.
For snow. The rest. For something other than the possible.
Something other than the fog. Settling as thorns. Frozen.
On fences. Winter, in its subtlest arrival, barbs our barriers.
Still. No one misses the ordinary. Not even the blackbirds.
Just as no one, on either side, misses the end of the world.

SAFE HOUSE (FOR LACK OF A BETTER TERM)

If I strip myself of everything—what's left is not

the pressure of the cardboard gun on my mother's temple
or the sharpied note transcribed for bullied fingers
or the shoelace lost and tied to its chilling looseness
or the wordless fatherhood in rows of garden beds
or the family truths on a taped-over VHS cassette
or the rusted hook with cured cuts of madness
or the syringe golden between a set of steel teeth
or the ammonia jar welting a collapsed lung
or the darkness living under other people's names
or the unanswerable question no one ever made use of
or the undoings that are near impossible to trace
or the crease that tempers the notice to resettle

what's left is a pardon—the appetite of an overcast day

MAMIHLAPINATAPAI

1.

["they're seated. and earned their degrees in art history. they walk toward the dimly lit corridor"]

2.

["in other words, the logic of small satisfactions mobilizes its subjects toward a critique of our return to the old and new conditions of production. there's always a true enemy, a secretary who knows about the difficult work of changing a light bulb"]

1.

["revolutionary change, thousands of cardboard domes, mutilated bodies, spontaneous echoes and outbursts, smoking or drinking, to limit, to stand up, something that happens to those in the know, guilty and starving, what is money actually the root of, this performance, this property, these charges further confirmed, some hidden message, return to normal, sudden attacks, a to b"]

2.

["i sleepwalk the benzedrine dogs and return home empty-handed. i asked if he could have a few words with me, i mean literally. i'm thinking of the way showing no sign of emotion halts the trains in their tracks—or makes them drown in the inhaler's patented blue"]

1/2.

["it is this that hinders the passerby from complete surrender. the iron cast sculpture in the yard. the swing, garbage cans, barking dogs. the image of giant worms consuming your life. but your legs won't halt. driven by a madness that grows out of the television screen. they continue to run without discretion. without hesitance"]

At Burger King We Don't Eat

We sip flat Fanta through the same straw,
watch people lick mayo from their fingers.
Pop songs crackle through the speakers.
My thighs spread on red vinyl,
her skin is taut, dusted with fine blonde hairs.

In the Topshop fitting rooms
we have the maximum amount of clothes.
You're tiny. We change with our backs to each other.
She peeks at me sliding Joni jeans over my bum.
Me, at the dip of her back when she's changing tops.

Are you hungry? She shakes her head. *Me either.*
She takes a mouthful of ice
from the Fanta cup, sticks her tongue out.
I watch it pool, spill from the corners.
She runs her finger over her collar.

We leave the beach party early,
the sea a deep purple. We chase
the incoming tide across the pebbled coastline.
Vodka from the bottle in quick swigs.
The whole town behind us, glittering, ours.

When it gets dark, she caves. I follow.
We rip open paper bags and sprawl fresh chips
into one golden heap. Steal half-eaten Chicken Royales
and Whopper Burgers abandoned around us.
Ketchup on her lower lip, aftertaste on my tongue.

The man tells your daughter she looks grown up

She is thirteen, supple
and they want her.

Sophie

We're seventeen,
spending our summer
reading *Girl Talk*
under her parents' apple tree.
Sophie teaches me to kiss
with her lips, wet tongue
sliding over my back teeth,
her nails unravelling
the skin of my neck.
She teaches me how to take
a hand diving under
my bra: moan low,
back arched,
slicked curve.

I'm ready.
She holds my hand
all the way to the beach,
feeds me shots under the stars
until the world melts
and my voice is slow, slurred.

She introduces me to a boy
with acne scars.
He has me on his lap,
hand at my lower back
drawing slow circles.
His face, blurry double-take,
ground shifting beneath me.
He takes me to the woods.
I'm tripping over my feet,

glowing at the moon.
You're so fucking drunk.
Look back,
Sophie's watching us,
waving.

I hold in my hand
Lady Satsuma

she has a glow to her
a flat-bellied weight
the sweetest dimples
stippling made
for the fingertips

the pieces of her
rounded thigh
crescent eye
fragrant hostels
for amnesiac glands
        for the nose
        a barbarian pop
        of redness, riding
        swooning
        on polyester
red has no place here
accosting this consecrated colour
orange is for worship

so, worship:
peel away, pretty veins
but keep the skin
smooth
it's too late
an afternoon
for sticky fingers
so:
prise open papal segments
tuck them in a box
go sit by a tree

she is with you
waiting
tilting the boughs
take out a segment
a curving crescent sigh
hold it to the light

see, she shimmers
and clutches it
in her humming core –
is the soul a thing to be touched?
a barbarian pop
orange this time
dribbling made
for the fingertips

if only you
were less like a moth –
but collisions stand
as murder at noon
orange is for murder
and

Lady Satsuma

this wind
dances around the bottle's top
singing as she goes

this same wind
flies whistling feathered kites
in sunny ceremony

a wind came all this way
to stead, to cool,
atop the world –
unfurl the sun
come barren, too,
for company, crooning
so hoarsely chasing
the rook

Simeon

standing against this litany
this first vomitus
of man
that contaminant of lunchtime
you will not know happiness

but then, some loves
have caves in them
some, with sardines,
beg you play the seal
at Calais
feed me sardines
lie, loved ones, clapping

but Prince winked at you
in LAX
where happiness
strolled nearby
and nobody knew either of you

this sagging city
drooping damp
this crook-necked chicken
a hovel to impulsion –
feed me love
and feeling
knock back love
and feeling
go forth only
with love
and feeling

Steve's Biography

How Queer I Live On Norfolk Coast

a sudden gust turns the reed bed
to whispering sea
the wind blows me
to wander lonely as a queer

to see all these trunks   thick to the touch
their exposed skins glistening
I belly slide along muscular arms
become bird   lizard   caterpillar   crepuscular squirrel

to gaze down on village people
tourists cruising   daddies hammering pegs
erect tents to camp   out in the sticks
duckies   otters

foxes   flies   free ranging cocks
bushes   cottages   pansies   dirt tracks   dykes
everything always opening
everything always coming out

Gardening

in Sheringham   I have a small cottage
garden that spills onto the shingle beach

the only wall that borders it is horizon
I plant pansies   tie dyed roses

green carnations   violets
rainbow wall flowers

I want Creeping Charlie to over run
flora   take up space   coalesce   create

new forms   in my Eden   I'm God   Mother
Nature   no one forbidden entry   fruit

Inosculation

inosculation is
a natural phenomenon

in which the trunks   branches   roots of two trees
grow together

it's most common
with trees of the same kind

the branches first grow separately
in proximity to each other until

they touch
then bark

abrades away
as the trees blow in the wind

they self-graft   they grow together   expand
ambling alone through High Kelling woodland

I clock tree carved cave art   your names in hearts
GS   GG   1997

were you two boys   both penknife sharp
who met in this woodland just to explore

did you find shelter in each other
did your trunk's inosculate

limbs bending around one another
I kiss your names   I hug your hearts

October

Oracle Bone

A mere wedge of burnt scapula-bone
would have served an oracle of the Shang

dynasty. One such would have sat alone,
with time enough to smoke whole forests

of green tea with silver jasmine, tooling
porous ox relics and tortoise carapace.

With these he could rehearse fortunes
from the clefts in the tortured staves.

Tourists come to see him, shillings
flipped to the organgrinder. Somewhere else

a curtain is drawn back, a fire lit. Painted girls
turn china cups, and turn them again, while here

nerveways and memories are cut back
into the shell that forsook them; his fingers

curled with custom, his eyes unfixed
as flecks of gold leaf in a cold saint's cell.

Walker

For you every step was a carnival. You wore
the idea of yourself in harlequin:
the mismatched patches of iodine swabs
and plaster-gauzes, the Russian-doll masks

of your funny-faces, and a proclivity to vanish
behind arras drawn smooth and blue
as a hospital bed's curtain. You made the children
dance to the pell-mell of your automaton clock-

work. Performing, you were a craft in neon,
a circus-tent for skin. You loved the curious
choreography of canned laughter, the sudden apocalypse
of event, the switch-blade-language of properties.

You embraced the literal in plastic: the implausibly
yellow banana-skins you winked at in your path,
the trick-carnation's squirts you excused
for your tears, guns firing 'Bang' to stop hearts

dead, the collapsible keg, and satires of bodily
functions. Your run had a story too. It taught us how
you learned to live without the gravity of flesh.
What was this naked being in earnest when

you quicksilvered at the pull of the tight-rope?
And how they cheered. Your encore was a stillness
that was all approximation, each limb baffled
in a probability of place, and the audience applauded

one last time. When you performed, my dear,
there was never an empty seat in the house.
What do they stare at now with such a hungered grace?
To whose show do they go when they can no longer

fever your thoughts with their looks? Who clowns his foot
for their amusement? But then there are the days
when in the dark of an unportraitured wall I see
a painted grin, shark-teeth, your eyes' deep hypnoscopes;

I hear again the arcade's song, the dank accordion,
the crude drum-roll before the freak comes on,
and I am overjoyed to feel your gloved hands reaching
through to catch and catch and clasp, shark-teeth gnashing.

I Am Your Brother

My death was a quantity.
It filled me in stages.
I was a witch, a cutter, a queen,
I was your brother.

I'm sure you loved me
for you left me secret offerings
like I was a Tamarind spirit-tree,
hanging tooled autopsies,
glass eyes, and baby-shoes

from my dry branches.
When they laid me out,
they marvelled at my maternity.
My heart was an amniotic bag.

A self-embracing thing
still moved inside. You see,
I never lost myself completely;
though I was a burial, a terrorist,
a mask, I am your brother.

The Possession

You've not taken to spitting raw cuts and coal,
brass pins and wire elements. Here's no satanic
yoga, nor machinery of thrown voices. You've slid

into possession the way a seagull finds its furrow
in the slipstream, inhabiting the drift of the earth's
habitual needs. Your possession is not an invasion.

(Keep it quiet. This is our secret). It turns the light-bulb
into a muscle pumping photons into your external
organs, keeping here a commode alive, there a pack of pills

breathing, knotting your nerve-ends to your bed.
The thermometer on the wall is a silver gland, endlessly
swallowing and secreting against the hard fever

of the world; and your face is now a wholesome swirl
of rootless stems and seeds, now a voodoo mask crumbling
with wood-rot and worm, betraying no trace, no human

memorandum, of anything you need to love. Brother
I have learned so much. How can I thank you
for your possession which transforms me still still still?

The Russian doll

1

item from the sound archives

fuck off   I'm not exhibit A
we're not a fucking roadshow

a rope and two mules
twins   Sarcy & Sulky   adolescents

2

Mr Big Himself
Bully-Boy-Bastard
Fucktator

such names are like small tropical fish to a koi carp

Perpetrator has a tough job   can never retire   will he mellow
with age

only once   outside the Whitworth
did we catch X off-guard

I understand
one of us / some of us said
you're also an exile

3

careful I always am / she often is
when handling knives
hold on to the handrail Metrolink platforms
use that right hand

volunteer anonymous already has a medal

4

mother's legs tango flamenco dancing on tables taking
risks
gets out of danger by losing a leg nickname mother gave proves a
blessing
little spider's head

5

mostly the cuckoo sits frozen inside the clock
its song is borrowed probably Schubert

Age: 3+

6

has the Russian doll on permanent loan

the one herding the cats

Depth

regarding my right leg

this is a foreign country

for which I will need a visit visa

Heart of Darkness with Kurtz

is a book   not a destination

dark water   leaking boats

somewhere around now the river deepens

Safe house

Where will it be? What will be inside?

you already know if you are living in this small space a cardboard cupboard that
even the best of lives are flammable

the strawberry box of memories
Dave Brubeck's *Take Five*

at the end of the line someone will be waiting for you
someone to whom you have ties their shoulders are a temporary saloon

the picture of the ice cutter from Alaska a few
small men on the ice coloured anoraks

singing is escaping so fast no-one can catch you Scarlatti as
a rope ladder over the abyss

photos a card her Venetian mask
a fire blanket in the kitchen

don't follow the first instruction until you have examined it closely it may be
something metal from which you can only escape by removing yourself from your
limb

a coffin of white wood
(bad people would not think to look inside)

the narrow old blue chair that holds you

a ginger cat but not called Louis
that name is taken

the only safe house is time about 6:30 the long golden shadow the voice of the
person who kept you safe when you were small

Motto

my motto is *let's go*
even rain makes for a happy day
as rain is water   all my days
start in the shower   I may sing
as songs are water
I'm just going where the day goes
and when the day turns
it's glorious   going
into early evening
and   if I'm not by water
I once was and will be again

The Coin

All women become like their mothers.
That is their tragedy. No man does. That is his.
— Oscar Wilde

Nevertheless, I breeze through the world's emporia, equipped
with titbits of finely diced life, whiffled under servers' noses:
hummingbird-raptor, hunter of chatter. I flit between tills,
hands not reflected in their counters. My mother's grip
lingers on receipts like a lifejacket, longing to thumb-flick

a crumb, a morsel, bait. Now, I go into the cut-price
smiles of chemists and butchers with intent:
conjure snippets with overwrought gestures,
offer a coin to every stranger,
daring them to flip it.

To the River Stour

some call you *S'toor*, like *poor*
and I thought this your proper
posher name because mum
pronounced you that way

others called you *St-our*, like *our*
and maybe that's your name
too as you wiggle like an idyll
on a National Trust postcard

through Essex-Suffolk floodplain
horizon   pinned on with spires
punctured by telephone masts
ears trained on each glottal stop

coppiced willows flank your banks
boaters meander as they squint
to find tributaries into Constable
gorgeous and serene so flat and yet

I longed for the wide mouth
of estuaries   the way they aren't
one thing or another   their brackish
manner   part-play   part-threat

Stour, *St-oor*, *St-hour*, you're a Site
of Special Scientific Pinterest
a keepnet for Nordic walkers
a cowpat for bluebottle tourists

and streams of gleaming Land
Rovers yearning for a blemish
a picture-perfect cream tea
on an English patina, cracking

While Mum Describes Her Side Effects

my sequin vest revolves in the machine
and messages ping from distant siblings.

We're all on a crash course in terminologies,
studying lymphocytes and subtexts, remotely.

A brother on WhatsApp jokes about stem
cells putting down carpets, before they select

wallpaper, making themselves at home.
As the vest revolves, the round door becomes

a glittering cross-section, a fabulation, a diagram
of her bones, something magic now inside them.

This numinous matter zapped from a donor,
swirling until the programme ends, our

mother emerging, fresh. In the meantime,
we're in Yorkshire, Madrid, adrift in time

zones: all of us trying to feel at home.

I want someone
I can just
be myself around

♥

I want someone
who will literally
tear me a new arsehole

♥

I want a relationship
that lasts more than
eight weeks

♥

I like a bold
pubic
region

♥

I like a big
like a gym
like a big gym goer

♥

I'm going to see
if I can squeeze a bit
of life out of him

♥

He's so funny
so funny
like, not quick-witted
but so funny

♥

A lot of people
spend a lot of time
overthinking things
but she doesn't do that

I don't want to have kids
with someone where I feel
like I'm doing everything

♥

One of your hairs
is on my pastries

♥

There's a few little red flags popped up
in the last couple of days but
they're only *little* red flags, so

♥

It doesn't make
any sense
at all

♥

Did I
jump in
too quickly?

♥

Oh mate I'm calm
I'm calm I'm calm
I'm calm

♥

Ugh
cats

♥

Missionary?
That's boring
like eating a cracker
without butter

I don't do that
I'm not that girl
I won't laugh at you
to make your dick feel bigger

♥

He wanted to blindside me
with shitty personal comments
for me the whole thing
feels like a shitty cheap shot

♥

I don't do
fiery girls

♥

You're
a strong
woman

♥

I think
I literally was
a placeholder
blue-tacked to
someone else

♥

I'm not going to lie
this tastes
really fucking weird

♥

There's a new girl
coming in and she could
fuck shit up

Prayer

after Alasdair Mac Mhaighstir Alasdair

God bless
this sea-vessel,

which from the very first day,
it seems, was shouldered
by Clanranald. Lowered to the bay,
our war-torn heroes are heroes
beyond war, beyond the gale
and the ghost-note of air;
far out beyond incisive breakers
shattering over a rocky shore,

may you, sacred
cubed God,

harbour us, moor us to the hush.
It was you flooded earth
and pressed into cardinal points
a compass of wind that skirls
after all. So keep us, father,
our kyle-slicer and steel,
craft and crew, in your safekeep.
Sails, rigging, anchor, rudder.

Fix our tackle
like your only son

to the mast, a seaborne crucifix,
and each mast-ring also
that secures the sail-yards and all
the moss-fir and heather ropes

be blessed: halyard and stay
flawless as you refuse us
our failure, our drift off-course.
Cartographer of every berth

under the sun, we bask
in your direction.

Lichen

Life is blemished and golden
moonglow, a lichen borne of love,
the fruiting body you did not become.
Or did you? We couldn't keep you
hidden in the tussocks of panic
forever, but when you kicked,
fifth instar to a shimmering
green, you were still our little secret.
You quickened into life and through
your mother as she began to darken
with the days: hips to belly button
enclosed a faint line, smile mottled,
a mask cracked into mosaic,
and all during the first trimester.
Too early. I said we're too young.
Never said I was
afraid, but I was. So afraid
I couldn't hear what your mother was
afraid of, this being her one chance.
I didn't see, didn't see
behind surfaces of lichen-grey
overgrowing everything
what you were meant to be: summer's
day-flying butterfly, our mountain ringlet,
rare in your desire for montane air.
Instead you were turned to script lichen,
forked, curved letters no one would believe,
not even me. When the floor
revealed you were bloodspot lichen
I knew what I had done.
Even now, six years since your mother and I
rinsed our fingers clean, I still liken you
to chrysalis, a black word. Black after green,
after regret. The wound death brings
is the afterlife.

Heil Valley

Field run to seed along the grain
of granite, trees under dusk and ruin
complete any piecemeal dark.
Blacker than char, a squirrel angles
toward pitched meadowland, listens
for anything else, an owl
concealed by shadow, or far off,
fast through the canyon that never stops,
the wind-splitter, a motorcycle
dying into night. Nature's sonographer
with big probing ears, it can read sound
as well as hear. Watch how it scans
woodsmoke for a seasonless year
high among the pine-fork, then re-builds
its needle-stitched cup, cache that was
brimful with seed, berry and acorn,
until it realizes nothing
discerns nothing after wildfire, after
the aftermath. Only loss, and worse
the evergreen of memory is reversed
to never-green, a nothing-nest,
so eerily similar to nothingness.

November

when a go is what they give you

i had to get vouched for to get inside.
if i could get vouched for i could go on in,
go overboard, go all in, go across
the windswept ocean. i dropped my eyes:
they watched unblinking as the door swung shut
behind a great divide now bridged. the disparity
absorbed in silence. a face that did not belong.

i never brought it round again. i dropped
the frightened whisper - tried a lisp instead,
a different laugh, a thinner lip, tried to pass,
a destiny apparent in all the ways i kept
on trying to get inside though i had got an in,
as if required to model how i wanted
to be seen, the way they never would.

they loved to see me itch to bounce.
they kept me brooding, kept me tethered
to my colour, mispronounced and out to sea
where they could watch me drowning.

this is the bruise i have uncovered; the years
i spent entombed and lonely in that green
unpleasant land, their every need a fresh
demand, and no one ever told me different.

i worked as if a farmer ploughing his own field,
as if the crop was mine and by it i'd be fed,
but i was an ox, instead, harnessed tightly in the yoke.

all that carry on we carry

the quid pro quo of purity and right is always telling on itself:
it lends itself as aspiration and example - the jewel stays
on display, the gun stays trained abroad and in the city, centred,
to brutalize and exploit in both your adjacence and objection.

i had my function as a member of the company. i marched
beside my brutish mates; they loved a royal skinful. i learned
how i might kill myself because i was awful eager. i broke
my back to keep up with the deadly mission, a skillful student,
but one without the rank enough to catch the competition.

i never once got close enough to feel like i was close to even.

i got filled up with all the nerve of i don't need your shit no more.
i brought my shit instead, but all my shit was shit i'd brought
from home, all that foreignness, that absent feeling in the body,
that frozen alloy in the bone, the blood congealed and muscles
petrified, firm enough to step in stride and stay untouched in motion,
a distance always safe enough, that kept enough away, that killed
the feeling in all the ways i was ice inside and nothing even mattered.

we get transformed once we conform to fit the patriarchal mask.
the performance of our task is acting out and always in reaction
to what there ain't time nor reason for, nor profit in interrogating.
this is the duty we each pay. we give all the beauty of what arises
in us for the power of an anaesthetic drive, the insult thrown at us
that then becomes ours to use in turn, and don't it feel so good
to use, so good to sing that song as old as their recorded time.

i never guessed the history held inside. how far back was i
supposed to go when everything inside came from somewhere
that they had sought out to enlighten? i couldn't shake the guilty
burden, as if i owed myself to the load, for having had the chance
to cash out one time, just one time, and just a little some.

twenty twenty

i've been six foot one apart from you
for more than thirty years. i was unprepared
to witness the uncreated and unbroken
movement of you entered into. i departed
time and time again, unseen, behind the line,
reacting to the notion you were never mine,
that what you'd felt i could not bear. i bore
the world instead, that smiling, caustic cruelty,
that exhausted politic, that killing for an overhead,
that kick directed down.

and then i heard you cry.
a sound composed not of seconds nor the silence
in-between but of a montage of the pieces i was not
allowed to feel. the pieces held in place, your
wilfulness at last restored, your little head at rest
upon my shoulder, your glowing face pressed
in my neck. your breath a puzzle to be solved,
your pieces of performance that i held: the feeling
that the war was over - for i could see myself at last,
and while nothing here will bring the stage set down,
no bolt of lightning will lay it bare and i remain
here with the set still standing, with no dramatic thing
occurring, now you and i are together in the warmest
correspondence. and all i hope is that we pass away
the way of nothing left to do, but hold you in my love.

the unfree versus

the stove got hot just one time and was kept
in mind as being hot forever. the system built itself
from that first time to make a stranger of the self.

they call it lost in thought for a reason, the reason being
our need to look up to the frontal lobe in awe, to keep
in mind the line that defines it as the lowest ceiling;
to keep me here above, and me down here, below,
asundered, an x against the question y, a little plot
of feeling gone awry, an illegality - the wave of correlation
describing no relation but the distance between me and reality.

please hold. i think i'm on the other line. let me put
you through. the ringer sounds like you, if a little older.

no one dreams of ending up a piece of shattered glass.
but here we are, all scuttling past like there were none
transgressed and never a transgressor. every window's
boarded up and we're just peeking through, forever,
always tense, kept on guard against transgression,
until it comes and we hold it off, feeling in our hands
held overhead as if we are engineered to be offhanded:
the wave gets dealt with and redacted, unhanded
by the strongest hand to hand it off somewhere.

it goes unfelt that way. it stays unsaid and we part ways,
inoculated in all the ways that we have learned to disappear.
so off we go in search of cure, as if the search itself
could be the cure, as if there were a cure or any ailment
but this holding off the rise that builds inside us as a wave
and swells with promises to pass - but stays forever cresting,
pearled in frost, withheld, held off, hold back, hold out, forget it.

this is the unconscious reaction that dams the tributary up.
everything determined by anxiety, bearing arms against our being
caught unarmed again beneath the ugly weight of memory.
we keep ourselves at arm's length, deprived of our felt sense
in preference for a glassy commonality, the painless way
we have of suffering without feeling.

i had the sensuality
of a youthful soldier's corpse. i gave my arms; they bore,
disarming - hurt held far enough away i could give it just enough
to seem to give it up sometimes.
it got hard to breathe, sometimes,
for all that i could never feel, for the killing of the daily quota,
the lightning burn, the lyric torn from my clenched tight, my fight
for air, the fight to keep my fight forever on the down low, my voice
denied its natural range to wander, these sorry little bird-like bones
that held the wave after wave as if to preserve the sense of somehow being
alright; these little digital hooks confined to slave for hypnotizing
a held body in its endless quest for safety. the absence of any safety
or repose in always serving the quest to douse and soothe the fire
in the eternal question of living. these shaky little bone hooks,
holding fast the wave above my head as if they could forever.

The Unreal Woman Isn't Ordering Steak

Her ambitions aren't that high, and besides,
she never cared all that much for sinew.
But after years of boiled, of bland, of soft,
you don't want to know what she'd do
for a wedge of crispy iceberg or a thick
wheel of carrot. A scalloped cucumber
with waxy skin would send her into fits
of glee; she has lengthy fantasies starring
escarole. But breaking through the fiber
would require mastication, and the firing
of muscle fiber itself would want for the pop
of neurotransmission, for the hiss and fizz
in each receptor and as it fired to life: too
many variables, each one over-determined
to fail. She sips water to dull her hunger.
She'll just have a coffee, thanks. Coughs
to cover the rumble of her stomach,
douses her mug with cream to stave off
the coming blood-sugar crash, the temple-
throbbing headache. No, she's *not*
hungry. She repeats it until it feels true.

The Man Who Punched Me in Seattle

Wore a red sweatshirt that made his fists
look like a child's, poking out as they did
from Hanes ribbed cuffs. Hardly the kind

to make a woman reach for her pepper spray:
no incoherent ranting, no sneaky grope in a hall.
Just a stubbled man, at middle age, with nowhere

better to be. As the cushioned tip of my cane
sucked itself to concrete in my shuffle-step walk,
he waited until I'd stepped just past him

to wind back his arm and land a knuckled lob
at my shoulder. What syllable escaped me
when my hand turned loose my purse

and the contents of my bags scattered free,
my arms flapping *hello-goodbye* for balance?
And did it harmonize with the crack

of my kneecaps on the ground, first one,
then its bony other, with the aluminum ring
of my adjustable cane jingling like flung coins?

It must not have been what he'd imagined,
the unseemly stretch of slacks in a crouch,
my jacket scrunching up under the arms,

the messy rumple of hair flapped forward.
He shook his head, a wet chuckle bubbling
on his lips. "I wasn't trying to hit somebody

with a cane," he said not to me.
Head cocked like a pigeon's,
he waited, as though for apology. "That,"

he said, jabbing a finger at the tangle
of limbs before him, my arm stretched for the cane
beyond my reach, "That is just my luck."

On Gravity

I.

A census of objects I have dropped:
knives, blade down and wiggling into floors,

unsheathed markers—permanent—on carpet,
The raveled threads of conversations.

Keys, repeatedly, bending each time at the waist
to gather them. Words I knew yesterday.

Boiling pots, dumplings and all. Hardcover books,
their covered corners into fleshy tops of feet.

The children of friends.
Friends.

II.

Objects in a vacuum fall at the same rate—
boulder the same as a feather or mateless sock.

Your body. Mine. If, in a vacuum, my grip gave way,
would you drop to the ground with me?

Would we come crashing to the pavement
at the same rate, both bruising knees?

We do not live in a vacuum. We swim in a chamber
pumped with air, with particulate and noise

which slow us, buoy our gobs of matter in deciduous
rotations: bodies spin, tossed according

to the manner in which air currents hook at planes.
If you are lucky, with many angles of cellulose,

you fall at the rate of the downy, furred leaf.
I drop like a bullet shot into mud.

III.

Force attracts us, we two in our bodies.
If our bags full of guts and nerve contain

all the same space and arrangement of particles,
our gravity holds each other at the same millionth

of a Newton. But I who am smaller, I who shrink
—and seemingly daily—spin toward you,

your gravitational pull going to work
on my lacey bone and thinning skin.

Will you notice the force you exert
as I collapse into your orbit?

IV.

But gravity moves both ways. It is not simply
the drag of earth that pulls mass home;

We too heave the earth toward self.
Shrinking the gap between us and ground,

our movement calls the world forward. We do not
accelerate alone—the ground itself rises

to catch us. But we are small bodies,
not intergalactic chunks of rock

hurtling toward a ditch. We'll never notice
when it happens, that shudder of molecular dust

as the soil itself anticipates a fall, readies
a spot, just body-sized, in waiting earth.

The ground will rise to gather us all,
but it catches some of us sooner.

Etymological Note

Before the seventeenth century,
the English language had no noun
for *comfort*. No way to describe

that state of better-off-ness
for sleeping on a bed of hay
than on a bare plank. No word

to express how much that hay's
texture might be improved
without the creep of insect

or midnight scuttle of mouse.
Comfort was only a verb—to solace,
to strengthen, to give what aid

or blessing one could against
a hemorrhagic wound or lung
splitting with rot. To be

comfortable meant nothing beyond
able to bear someone else's idea
of help: the smoke of censer

at prayer, the crumbling wafer
of last rites—bodily gestures
that lead a spirit into the dark.

When the nurse cracks the door,
the thin wedge of light raking
at my eyes, reminding my body

that it is body still, she asks if I
am comfortable. I say yes, reach out
my silent hand for touch.

A dream

One day I went for a walk-through Al-Saray souk, Baghdad's old bazaar. In the back of a shop stifling with dust, a painting caught my eye:

On a secluded beach,
Shredded limbs,
An empty chair,
A weary shell!

It was apparently a portrait of a half-veiled woman lying on the sand and rubbing her navel with her slender fingers.

I looked at it more closely. I found that in the face of her distress, the diaphanous breast flooded with blaspheme, the flesh seemed so vile that the dust lost its importance.

A horseback afternoon

I was afraid of falling dead all of a sudden, just like that. But this thought was quickly abandoned, and I began to worry: what had happened to my father, why is he late, we were supposed to meet here in front of the windows of the Orosdiback galleries: he promised to buy me a suit. For tomorrow is the first day of the Eid; I must put on new clothes in order to earn everyone's respect - especially of the girl I've been after for a month. What had happened to him? Half an hour has already passed. The second hand of the watch runs on, doubling the intensity of my worries. People come in and out, in perpetual motion. I turned left and right, there was no trace of my old man. I wonder if, once again, he had wandered into the vineyards of the Lord. A large hourglass, displayed in the window, captivated my gaze as the silica flowed into lower bulb, down to the last grain. I saw that the department stores close early, as they did every holiday evening. Here is the last customer just leaving, the curtains are falling and the lights abandoned me one by one. Darkness enveloped me and the echo of my footsteps was the only thing that resounded in my head all the way home. When I arrived, I went to my room, and to my surprise, I saw a gray suit on my bed, along with a sky-blue shirt and a banknote to spend! In my sleep, I saw myself in a carriage with a girl on the way to Roxy cinema which was showing a Marlon Brando's film A Street car named desire.

Beneath veil

I remember how,
That day,
In the evening,
Your body comforted me.
I never saw you veilless,
It was spring,
The cold far from us,
The sun coating the beach
With a smile of old times
Its rays spread under the sheets!
The words clashed against the waves
While our lips ran
To quench their thirst
And our bodily souls
Bathed in fantasies,
Floated in the elliptical attraction of the depths!
I took a drink of your body, filling my lungs.
And the knowledge spills
Across the pages.
I think of you once more.
I see you lying on the sands that shine like starry skies!

I remember...
I feed on my memories of you
I drive through the folds of your absence
You are the appearance of all that illuminates.
Love has only one form: your body!
I loved you, I love you
And after all this
I will love you much more than before
No matter if love
Is nourished only by the delights of evil
And dies in monotony,
In the passionate tide of scandals!

Words eat raw

… Even now, I try to make sure this attempt was successful. Without it though, the streams of reflection would have been lost.

The poem stumbles in front of this sudden deadlock which never closes its eyelids. It consciously follows a thought, un occult amalgam of language, that clashes with its own hallucinated discoveries. A fleeting enjoyment. I began to bang against the walls of the unconscious, so violently that blood spurted from my head. At that moment my mouth became the crater of my thoughts. Words came out recklessly, piercing the sheets piled before me: dissolute vocables, odorless. I cannot underestimate the effusion. It appears to me as a scene crossed by a prophesy, surfaced by the illusion of seeing the very act of writing. The sheets are being sucked into a maelstrom of what was going on in my head. Notes scribbled here and there. I hear their whistle. I contain their wheat. Each paragraph is an orchard and the meaning a resting place.

My thought, reflection of a being hidden in the depths of time, appears in this moment of creation, as the groaning expression of a sensory experience that rises and falls.

Everything passes through and participates in the immensity of space: the place, the time, the houses, the elements… So many secrets remained buried under the meaning, unseen to the eye of modernity. Yet, aged secrets are as empty of significance as the orbits of the dead, pale objects that soon crumble under the shock of revelation and unrealized consequences. At the lightning's calm, the sleeping world whizzes. To write is to shatter the closed window of the internal. It is to launch a cry and run into the night.

Yes, the image will come one day, and we will make love on a bed of clouds and clays. Stick to your obsessions and to your breath, the rhythm inside you. Another truth, energetic, will rise from the nostrils of the immediate!

Poetry, the oxygen of man, its desires can be satiated by its mediums, the words, when they reclaim their right to run freely through the threads, roses and chains... Words consistently state what they convey. Automatic revelation. Human beings live by words. In fact, we are alive only within words. Only words remember us. The ego is part of the word, and their framework is speech. We utter words before they give us tongue…; to such a degree, that we make them hollow like the void where everything gets buried and forgotten. The forgotten, this deluding *unmastered past*, does not die out. It always peers through each breath, each image like a returning ghost. It is necessary to work the stone of the image.

I like words bristling with the dewclaws of a fierce rooster. They sound like rain, release lightning in the heart of darkness. They raise the magnitude of the contemporary man, reviving, from all directions, his imagination and set him in revolt. While exchanging confidences in celebration of the ephemeral, words like cats, escape from the cage of the lexicon… and stray away into the unknown.

Rise up narration, get involved in the riot of words where the lips get wet.

Reality is a beast that walks cautiously on the wastelands of survival. It cannot return to itself without a swig of utopia, a shiver that runs through the realm of necessity.

I see, from a suspended boat, trembling shores.

A hat whitens foolishly and flies into the void.

I kick the names of the past.

I chose life.

From afar, it seems that a blaze awakens with a slap of flame the exact image.

The first ovules surge, leaving sleep. They communicate to us what their compeers, the poets, were simmering. Thought do not always lose sight of language. It braves the memory.

Here is the syntax unmasking the face of the grammar.

Here is the bird of ambivalence in search of a protective doubt.

Hither and thither the effusion…

Word is Other within each of us. The dream, it tells, unites us.

To avoid confrontation and feel the truth being born in your mouth, all you'll need is to awaken the gang of mirrors.

Poems are not Pavlovian dogs, aesthetic salivation, but mental explosives to blow all the walls. Drink from the poets' vessels, and you will feel their light bursting upon you.

The dawn, always standing, falls in pieces like a memory ready to confess and to unload its bag; landscapes, horizons, and ruins flying on the sheets.

The poem points to the ultimate debacle at the door of the poet.

Writing is digging through the wall of language to catch a glimpse of the secret life of the word.

mixed herbs

in your Italian food
some used to be
toxic operators
plants
used to conspire
some store
more ammunition
in the vaults
some doesn't enjoy
Mozart
some have
tooth sensitivity
but the gun
appeared long ago
in any case
there will be exogamy imposed
by the
extraterrestrial
human explosion
in molar and molecular
space-sense

provisionary plant anxiety

I live in the dark for years
sometimes, followed by
a flood before a draught thatshakesme
from top to toe. I understand
there's a crisis. I shut myself up.
Perhaps it's already
dark outsideIdon'tknowI don'tknow.
Shoes here. Feel my feet frozeninside
wherever they are.
Can't.Shoesneveroff. Mightescape.
SweatFlood.
shoes send me messages from below -
[…]
I know I can never afford sunshine, ever.

Hello

Thank you for buying me
peonies. Otherwise I'd think
my female body is worthless
and that you won't offer me anything
for doing unpaid household chores.
Now everything's complete. I'd rather
be algae in my next life, swimming
eternally in the ocean, part of the
moss community that doesn't
excite anyone;
or a medusa, hair made
of seaweed which can escape
the life on earth.

Sending snakes xx

False Protagonist

In the unforgiving light of
the bread aisle, / I admit I've
asked questions above/ my
councils' leavened wisdom.

Collagen is not a problem /
for bread, is it? More of a
statement, / they sit there
expressionless, beautifully
risen. / Such good listeners.

Mostly, given their proclivity
towards structure, / I ask
about purpose: what
happens to the roots/ of
felled wheat? Do they
remain tangled/ in the
earth's darkness, thirsting?

Bread finds abstraction like
this bewildering. / I tell
them of equal measure:/ a
woman, barely a woman
really, / grown peripheral /
to her own story.

Middling: a soliloquy

bullshitfriendlyneighbours	middleagemiddleclass	donotwakethekids
snottysleevesnosnacks	illfittingdresses	weekendsathome
spousalmicroagressions	impostersyndrome	paychequetopaycheque
deadendcareer	iregrethavingkids	skintagsouvenirs
datenightantithesis	frumpyattire	parentchildmatchingoutfits
currentbehaviourcringespiral	notimeanxiety	thesaggytitshow
midweeksobriety		mykidsknowthepasswordtomyphone

Those two years: a portrait

start with the hairline, apparently./ treat it as abstraction: a cliff or a coastline/ would be obvious./ a garden border is too, although/ explosions of pampas grass/ like your temper.

so much fuss/ so much meaning attributed/ to the eyes./ paint them as strawberries,/ and think about all the people thinking/ about the meaning of strawberry eyes.

lips move/ practising the act of speaking. colour them/ a cherry red/ because this is the shade you think all grown women wear./ the language you are inhabiting/ is the way you think all grown women speak./ also at this time, you consider the height of glamour to be sips of Diet Coke/ between long drags off a Camel Light for breakfast;/ a lipstick-stained butt.

waves crash out of ears./ that white noise can be felt to this day,/ soothing - like the sounds permeating through the partition wall at night.

you rethink the eyes, acknowledging that strawberries/ were an annoyingly coy thing to do./ they should be black as your sister's first boyfriend's/ – the one who beat her./ paint them as ink stains because she hid it like you grew up in a family of violence;/ because it was so not obvious/ obvious, in hindsight. Your guilt is an ink stain/ for always making this about you.

hell, paint the nose job you wanted;/ paint the smell of orange blossoms in early spring/ as if the whole world lived in the olfactory paradise of your childhood.

remember, angular features (e.g. strong jawline)/ = confidence and manliness (in goodies)/ = aggression and predatory behavior (in baddies)./ this means that, depending on the time of day,/ the portrait can either evoke positive traits (conscientiousness) or negative ones (neuroticism),/ or both simultaneously/ (e.g. an epic display of road rage whilst driving to visit your grandmother).

in the background, different versions of your signature,/ like a form of dress up/ because you had the time/ to endlessly graffiti – on notebooks, on trees and desks,/ on forearms.

there is a photograph of you at 15 looking like a boy/ there is a photograph of you at 17/ looking like a Barbie./ these will make you feel lesser for the rest of your life./ marvel at how, in those two years,/ everything seemed so slow-moving while you waited for your life to begin,/ while you lived your life/ like you were on horseback.

a winter sky of hot nude pearl
escape, escape
I have come here to heal

night roars quietly
I light a lamp and think –
of iron chains, memory, the city

its flora – beloved
I have snatched night
from darkness, from dust

*

in a flash my mind's eye shows me
a tormented existence
reflections, lies
a staggering mistake

the symbolic lovers
androgynous, inverted
the sweet anarchy of the body –
the body, sick

I have been deeply wounded

*

long sequences of light filtered
through the essence of dust –
sweet-smelling dust slaked with light
dust-red, dust-green, chalk-mauve

autumn inflaming the body
the flesh drunk-dark
shedding snatches of petals

hunt for nakedness
in those little cafes, the old poet
stirs under the petrol-lamps
disturbed by this desert wind

*

I had to come here to rebuild
the black ruins in metal
gold, phosphorous, magnesium
with slices of water-melon

in the open petal of the mouth
dusted by pollen kisses
lightly camphor-scented…

*

I am buried deep
in the shallow sand of madness
I believe in ecstasy, in suffering
I know, I know

*

in the quietness of the evening
the mind is licking its wounds
sulking along deserted beaches –
empty forever

grey cloud and shadow
wreckage washed up

*

alone, I have no name
I am cloudy, useless
wounded fragmentation
– breath, skin, voice –

the house answers in a language
of its own invention

*

I live alone, sick
hopeless and haunted
pale, blue-veined, sullen

I dream vulgar dreams
spaces between time
a tide of dead things
powerful and deliberate

*

white-robed figures
like scattered paper, ringing silver
hot red glimpse of half-sleep

torn rags of flesh, some hidden
slaughter, the moans of a love-
song ground to powder

tired and blinking into pale hot light –
flowers of anguish, bandaged dreams
soft sad days

*

I glimpse the sea – a dusty silver flood
plunge softly, softly into the light

how touching, how feminine, terrific
queens, man-eating cats, acts of dirty love

*

a rare nightmare full of exotic charm
I approach the supernatural

December

Tide against chewing
razor blue gums
salt in the wound
Citizenry amassed
dividends / dividuals
we were on the un-shore
of revocation'd privilege
in mere continuance.

The Acts
abolish you & I
did you not see warning signs?
Did you feel asphyxiated
In the conqueror's deluge [?]
we arrived un-a-breasted
of what they intended
cannot go back
marooned in land.

How many testimonies will we need
to hear before the truth
can cry out, unlaboured
by the discourse of non-position?

Who can speak for others?
It rests on the rear-glanced treason:
I am your seditious anti-national.

My entry is not an offering
& your palm is over my forehead
forcing words into the soft-bruise
of my voice which I can no longer stomach.

Ensconced in breathlessness
we moved in / as opalescence
ignominious fortitude there
after autochthony immured us on the kelp.

That territory takes fear into the ground
where I grasp what it is to be effaced
by the recoiling hydra
where the gesture reverses
& dispersal pulled back into the clench of a fist.

unheimlich radio you follow me around
with chalk as I lay down
as I laid down
on a private road holding white calla-lilies.

---

note on ius soli

fascist custom denounced as dated
embedded as secrets
with stamps on the bill
like caught marlins
lost in Cornish rockpools
revolutions kept us locked in-between
those same walls the government shot us against.

Pride in bunting or baked revelation
nostalgia ferments to hysteria
blockades on the imagination   where to now?
Home is un-safe and sea is the border.

In a shuttle movement
between text and context
abducted by identities that were prescribed to us.

Stuttering before
we meant to move into Right
welted by contusions in hachured zones of n'être

I want to make the meridian shiver into futures
tatterdemalion lightening
de omnibus dubitandem

This is the end of everything / the end has no end.

You've asked me if I'm real.
I have told you that I'm not real
that you aren't real
'cause if we're honest about it
you're asking them to recognise you
in a system that's erased both of us.
I fail to see how any recognition will suffice
or even lead to the level of social change needed.

You've told me to be pragmatic, non-judgmental
but how can I realistically acquire those qualities
in my longing for justice to materialise in the streets?
I want to know how your brain works so frankly
without attending to the scarified fossils of freedom
and taking no notice of how our flesh becomes object
or ignoring the absurdity of closing the door on my face.

You've already explained these things on-goingly
and I cannot fathom how repetition just breaks records
like how many people "*like us*" are hired by corporates
or winning a few prizes and meeting the monarch
when in the same movement a passport can be issued
so can a death, so can a loss, so can a person be unmade.

[Documentality as the chiliasm of intractable decreation–

What He Makes of Me

Little pointillist – he latches on wrong and takes
my blood for his palette, my breast for his canvas
and I am too sleepy to quibble. When I wake

there is a cuticle of bruise above my nipple
where his top lip crept greedy and drew
the blood through my skin in purple prickles.

His mouth, popped open in milky reverie,
is dreaming of bright red flavours to come.
I press the bruise and wince. It delights:

a stiff shirt collar grazing a love bite;
uncertainty on a week-day morning.
I wonder how much he has had of me.

This ruthless creation machine is his own
study in red and white, pink as a valentine.
He would suck the blood right through my skin
to complete himself and I would let him.

Born Free

Released back into the wild, she is uncertain. The instinct to feed is strong, but her infant is new to this. Patience is required. It is testament to the bond of motherhood that she perseveres. Many mammals faced at this early stage with such inept feeding might abandon their offspring. In this case, it seems to be a matter of the reward outweighing the pain and frustration of the initial struggle.

Dogged in his quest, her infant manages to get milk in his ear, in his left eye and on the far wall. A spot lands on the television screen, but is not fat enough to tumble over itself and run. She imagines herself rising to wipe it off, then turns her attention back to the business of establishing a good latch, to tickling this tiny stranger on the chin with her nipple, watching for the moment his mouth pops wide.

Plugged in, she nests in the long grass of the living room and watches endless documentaries about humans. Eventually, she picks up her book. One page in, she is faced with the problem of turning the page. She uses a combination of fingers, a knee and her infant's back to catapult the book to the middle of the rug where it stands erect on slightly fanned pages, inert, out of reach. She weeps, half-heartedly.

There is a noise in the long grass: footsteps. Someone enters. It is one of the humans from the documentaries, though this one is hunting neither for antiques, nor a husband, nor a killer. She holds her offspring close. The human bends with enviable ease, snaps up the startled book in one hand, returns it to her and takes her infant. She frisbees the book to the cushion beside her, holds her own hand. Waits apprehensively for her infant's safe return.

Glass, A Predicament

Isn't it bad luck, you ask,
to wear a dress of broken mirrors?
The seamstress is bullish

– *Nooooo!*
You are thinking of looking glasses.

You turn your head and the high collar
fingers up onto your cheeks,
splayed ice feathers, cut-throat razors,
testing the resolve of your skin.

You are thinking of dresses made of ladders!
she says. *Give us a twirl!*

You daren't. You can't.
You shift slightly and the fabric creaks,
smashed safety-glass, blanket of resistance,
a landscape of forced joints and grating folds.

You are thinking of dresses made of umbrellas
opened indoors!

Ought the ability to move not be prerequisite,
you say. How will I dance?
You lift an arm and the scraping
threads a cringe through your bones.

Forget dancing - can't you see yourself in this
walking down that aisle?

You stare in the achingly whole mirror,
imagine it – taking a step,
each tiny pane in the dress exploding,
sparkling the room in a galaxy of shards,
leaving you naked but for the backing gauze.
100% third act carnage.

I can see the whole world in it, you say,
and it is in pieces. Isn't it
bad luck? You ask again.

She says, *I don't know,*
are you the one who dropped the mirrors?

The Truth Machine

He stands like a little tin soldier in the front drive.
Why hasn't this been done before?
The lack of opportunity, I suppose,
between the coming of language and the departure of innocence.
I plug in the neon sign at his side and give it a dunt.
Its colours pop, an unnatural bloom.

From him, every reaction, every emotion, is truth.
For his smiles, he demands nothing.
There is no agenda, there are no preconceptions.
There is just the thing and the observer and the truth of it.
Primary colours, his emotions.
A spade is a spade, but oh my word – a spade!
Do you see how it digs? Think of the holes we could make!
Look at the shining line along its back
that moves when I move the spade – how does it do that?
A spade is all possibility and all beauty
and everything is a spade.

I can see the queues all the way from here to Slough.
Those who have never seen the truth.
Those who have had it and lost it.
Those who want to see the world anew, without its orbital debris
of tit and tat.

"Let's check he's working," says my Mum.
She pops 20p in the coin slot, kneels,
smiles and waits. He studies her face,
eyes tracing with care the journey of each wrinkle.
His neon sign flickers, then he speaks.

Butcher of Eden

Now God made Adam and Eve coats of skins and dressed them.
— Genesis 3:21

And when he was finished,
he scraped fat
from the backs of stretched skins,
wiped the blood,
sewed the seams,
bit the thread with teeth
and said:
Dress yourselves in these.

And they said:
what is this verb?
God shoved his knife into the earth, and said:
It's like make believe
but for your body.

And they looked at all the meat
still steaming
from when it was alive.
And God said: Eat,
and watched while
beasts of Eden fed
on beasts of Eden.

Feed the Beast

Back when I believed God would speak to me
God spoke to me,

and asked me who
I thought I was keeping happy.

I was keeping a six day fast,
feeding on fat and faith and failure,

and one evening, praying instead of eating,
worshipping what I did not know,

What I Did Not Know spoke to me
telling me to feed my hunger.

I was seventeen, or twenty, or forty five, or nine
and zeal was eating me alive.

When I heard the voice, I was sitting the ground,
wrapped around an instrument.

I had rid the room of imagery
believing that reading and not eating would be enough.

There was the sound of my stomach growling.
And the sound of nails scratching strings on a guitar.

There was the sound of whatever
made that starving beast start feeling.

The Underneath

The underneath. That was the first devil. It was always with me.
— Marie Howe

Here's the thing:

underneath the rage, the hurt,
underneath the hurt, the expectation,
underneath the expectation is hope in a something
underneath the hope there's hunger
underneath the hunger, a deeper hunger still.

I wake to an old story, and repeat it in the shower,
repeat it over tea, repeat it, amplify it,
put books into a bag, start up the car
and wait for the windows to de-mist,
I think about it at the junction, at the lights,
at the intersection, at the place where idiots make the same mistake
they always make while ignoring all the lanes placed there
to make us safe.

And underneath the story is a story,
underneath that story there is time,
underneath all time is memory,
and underneath all memory is a future and its questions.

I'm seized by an old dream. In it, I'm at speed,
but I'm not driving, no-one is. I'm on a train, an old one,
going underground. And I know I need to jump. I can see and I can't see
at all, there is wind and dark and terrible velocity, I know
that if I jump, I might die, but if I don't, I'll definitely
not survive.

Underneath desire is a hope to keep on living,
underneath the hope to keep on living is loss,
underneath the loss is my desperation for acceptance,
underneath that desperation is the belief that I am hateable,
underneath all that is fury and underneath the fury
is the hunter. Underneath the hunter is the hunt.

Act One, Scene One: Night

[*Lights up on the town already on stage holding its breath. Townspeople asleep in their beds etc. Chorus enter like fog climbing out of manholes.*]

Voices [together]: We are a chorus that moves like water

Voice 1: Daytimes we drizzle over playgrounds

Voice 5: and down the common

Voice 6: We get into hills

Voices [together]: We soak through ground

Voice 1: drain through the water table

Voice 5: coming up again in butler sinks

Voice 2: and toilet bowls

Voice 6: At night we drip through holes in human dreams

Voice 1: tune through sleeping heads

Voice 3: like a radio through stations

Voice 6: In stone houses and the council flats

Voice 3: we seep like water

Voice 1: watching dreams play out

Voice 6: across closed lids

Voice 7: And why watch?

Voices [together]: What else is there to do?

Voice 2: There's *literally* nothing else to do

Voice 1: but dribble through clean dreams of a vicar in his bed

Voice 6: or condense on long walls

Voice 5: in rooms above the sandwich factory

Voice 1: where men sleep two-to-a-pillow

Voice 5: dreaming Romanian dreams

Voice 7: We watch

Voices [together]: and that's all you need to know

Voice 6: And who is this asleep above the town

Voice 1: where the moor meets farmland

Voice 6: in a tent of wet nylon?

Voice 1: Their mind is quiet inside their skull

Voice 3: like the layer of cold water

Voice 7: at the bottom of a pond

Voice 5: What washes up on the shoreline of his dreams?

Voice 2: If you can call it a shoreline

Voice 7: Call it an edge then

Voice 1: Yes call it reeds

Voice 4: A name

Voice 1: What name?

Voice 4: Michael

Voice 5: Anything else?

Voice 4: a sister a daughter a kingdom

Voice 2: coke tins crisp packets

Voice 4 [channelling Michael]: *You know where you are with a mountain*

Voice 1: What's that?

Voice 4: *All things can be measured, maintained*

Voice 5: Shh, listen!

Voice 4: *The trick to raising a girl is*

Voice 5: Tell us Michael!

Voice 4: *to treat them the same as a boy*

Voice 6: Wait a second—

Voice 2: What?

Voice 5: Play that bit again

Voice 6: Spool it back to its beginning

Voice 1: and let it play

Voice 4 [still channelling Michael]: Water wakes me. Raindrops on nylon, dripping off the Douglas firs, twanging the guy ropes. I eat breakfast in the tent flap. Sausages, a soft white roll, watch the magpies pick through the car park. You know where you are with a mountain (I pack up the tent pegs, telescopic poles, knee out the groundsheet the best I can). I'm not interested in the high peak anymore.

Voice 8: Press your face up to the glass walls of Michael's dream

Voice 7: What do you see?

Voice 1: A hand shielding blue eyes

You could see us falling even then.

I'm wearing the net curtain from Premier Inn's window
like a veil. I'm eating Greggs from the bag.
All the people below the glass roof are
walking as though they are not incredibly small,
riding the mall escalators down from floor to floor
as if they're not endlessly falling. As if they'll never

wear no knickers and eat ring doughnuts
in front of an 8th storey window,
rolling gold zeros over the carpet.
The couples are holding minute hands, swinging
the club of their fists back and forth
knocking all comers out of their path.

The lighting in Premier Inn is particularly unflattering.
I'm unlikely to find true love again
in this light. If I turn it off, the pane flickers
from sticky-fingered mirror to city at night.
And the glass roof lights up like a yellow road,
staggering all the way to a gold, unveiled moon –

full and calm
as a guidance counsellor
giving nothing away.

Perdita

That day, I opened you up. Slid up your dress
and down your rough white knickers to find
a cavity in your plastic. A sprung hatch
like a submarine door / space-station airlock.
And inside: a tiny spindle, a switch clicking
uselessly; a moulded, purposeful void.

I took you down to Mother: once you'd held
a record player spinning miniature vinyl,
loops of laughter or gorgeous sobs, a mocking
comfort, replayed in play. Even, beating from
your belly, surreal jazz – birth-kick grooves.

Those records are outmoded, broken, misplaced,
and you have lost your voice. Your tipping blink
unsettled with a shake, I carefully re-dress you,
lift up my vest to press where my hatch must be.

At night, I replace you in the cot, a copy of my own
now long outgrown. *I'm here, I'm listening*, I say.
I hold and hold your plastic hand in mine.

I don't know what I'm writing about but

it's always wanting to know moss.
It's been impossible to get an answer.

Wanting to touch whenever it's secret,
on a low wall or behind a tree. To cry
into its unresponsive green pillows at night.
Never lie face down on a mossed stone at night.

Moss is the smell of hunger. I imagine a moss throat.
I recall pregnant mothers, stories of eating dirt.
You went through a lot of gherkins. We joke
about how sharp I turned out. Give me soft to eat.
Never lick moss off a grave. The dead are entitled
to a mitigation of stone. Besides, it's full of woodlice.

Moss bristles like a whisper. That's the sporophytes.
You sporophyte through my dreams, hinting and soft.
I can't decipher you, so I spend twenty-two years prodding.
Ah love, time to turn off the waterworks.
Moss can hold twenty times its own weight in water.

Perhaps the healing properties of bog moss,
recorded at the Somme – *"Mosses At War!"* –
were known to me all along, deep in my limbic system.

God! For a cool plaster of moss applied to the frontal lobe.
"…after a transient attack, patients may not respond
appropriately. Emotions may be felt but not expressed."
Take your forehead off that moss henge. This is a heritage site.

It's not that I don't know how to pray. It's just too much
like whispering into moss and missing the whispers of moss.

A doctor opens her briefcase. In place of a stethoscope,
there are two wads of sphagnum. Repeat into peat:
What does it mean? What does it mean?
What does it mean? What does it mean?

Moss's refusal to respond lacks all defiance.
It is always gently and fully occupied.

PROSE

January

teenage actress\

SHE HAS graduated from her initial freckle period to join the ranks of the superstars. Shriek, squeal, pout, strip off, it's a free for all from here. And who's gonna reap those big fat juicy rewards, baby girl? her father says, out of earshot of her mother and her mother's boyfriend. Us, that's who, and he poke-taps the flesh below her collarbone with one of his big sun-crinkled fingers. S'gonna be dreams comin' true time.

So whaddyou wanna be? her manager asks her.

Like… like, you mean like…

Like what *type*, she says. Sexy? Goodie-goodie? Geek chic queen? I can see you stepping into geek chic. I am *not* sure about this sweater, where did you get this? and she tugs the elastic-wool hem with a manicured finger. I like you in scoop necks. And more mascara. Remember the Just 7 shoot? The response to that is what we should aim for. Lotta influencer love for that look. You look flat, your core routine working out? Did Jay hit on you yet? He hits on everyone, he hit on me first session, I said if he did it again I'd cut his dick off. He hits on you, kick him in the scrotum. Unless you wanna fuck him in which case go nuts. Her fifteenth birthday comes and goes, her sixteenth. She puts keepsakes from the shoot in Sevilla around her room, in the house her mom bought with her money (she has learned not to refer to it as her money). Who's *that*? Janelle asks, pointing at the pictures of Juanito, but that's a secret, that one's just for her and the birds.

If she squints real hard with her eyes closed, she can see pools of light in the darkness—glowing neon red-yellow pools of love. It's cool to have a craft, she tells Dani, like I have this framework I can go to. Mm-hm, for sure, Dani says. Have I told you about the pool of love?

No,

Dani says.

Weeell, it's this pool that emerges from the inside.

When you've known true love.

Like, you can swim around in it. I like to backstroke.

Uh huh,

she says.

I like to dunk my head under in the moonlight and open my Goddamned mouth.

She gets the part, tells herself she'll just avoid the producer, not be in a room alone with him. She puts on weight because the Kraft services table becomes her safe place. Is that a *muffin top*? *Fuck* off Kayla. She entreats herself to try harder. She writes a poem:

> Where beyond the glimmer
> goes my heart?
>
> Where beyond the hearth
> that heats my castle
> goes my love?
> Wherefore drifts my love?

She entreats herself to try harder. She commits to learning Spanish. *¿Donde más allá del brillo entra mi corazón?* She looks out for scripts that might shoot in Andalucia. There is a pool, in Andalucia, that she visits, in her dreams, that she knows like the back of her eyelids. It's fringed with bulrushes, jacaranda, scree, and it is always glowing night, and the water is warm at the surface, cool to cold the lower you go, and dark, black, impenetrable—who knows how deep, she can feel it on the bare skin of her legs, her back, and he is splashing in the distant adjoined lagoon, singing

> *Mi amor va más allá*

The nomination is a surprise but won't hurt her prospects one fucking bit. You seem to have a real quality to you, the septuagenarian director tells her, and his spotless sidekicks nod nod nod. That's why we're interested in you. She adjusts her sitting position. Her mother's boyfriend is thumbs-upping through the window. The director assesses her lower body. Yes, he murmurs, yes, and the nodders nod. If you are sexy, you are the world's property, he tells her later, everyone has a right to you. You are Salmacis, you are Daphne… have you read the classics? No? Beauty, you see, beauty… it's so profound. We all must come to look. She learns to accept the things she cannot change, the hands she cannot see coming. She has, after all, her pool.

February

We were in a pub. A big group of us at a table, crisps, real ale, telling jokes, and 'should we get more crisps?'
Absolutely.

He was friendly, the bloke I had a wee next to at the urinal, wearing an Idles t-shirt. 'Good pub this,' we both agreed, but back at the big table after a couple more beers and exchanging life updates we started talking about the news and we all admitted we were starting to get a bit scared now. How bad was this going to get? I can't remember it being like this, ever. It was hard to understand what was going on in the news, even though I listen to *The New Statesman* podcast which is really good, but when every episode finishes I think, yeah I haven't retained any of that.

Even though the world felt so horrible I was actually feeling pretty good about things. I'd started seeing someone new, which doesn't happen often, and I was worried it wouldn't work out, but let's see how it goes. That's what I say about everything now, let's see how it goes.

Sometimes I look at my friends and think yeah, we are all getting really old now. That's what I used to worry about more than anything but now that it's happening, I don't really mind it so much. Look at them; my adorable chubby middle-aged friends. I've slept on all their settees. Oh getting older, it's really hard. I guess my sister doesn't realise how rapidly her baby grows ... but I see it, in her WhatsApp photos. He is so beautiful in so many different ways, my tiny nephew, who has the same name as my boss and it's been much easier at work since I've been talking to them in the same way. 'You're tired. That's why you're so grumpy. Would you like some banana? Don't get any on your tummy. Have you been up crying all night again? Your poor parents.'

One morning I was driving to work. On my last few journeys I'd thought this car doesn't feel right, I should definitely get it checked out at some stage, but I never quite got round to it. All the warning lights came on and I completely lost all power and the car completely stopped. Cars had to indicate and go round me. Hazards on, bonnet up, I just sat in the car completely distraught. I didn't know what to do. You know that feeling when something is entirely your responsibility and you don't know what to do. I just sat there, scared, confused. I don't know much about cars but I definitely felt this was bad. After about ten minutes another car pulled up behind me. This man got out and asked if I was okay?

I said ... no. Not really.

He said I don't know much about cars ... which wasn't exactly what I wanted him to say ... but he helped me push it to the side of the road so it was out of the way and he waited with me while I phoned the RAC. He said the same thing had happened to him, a few months ago he'd been driving across Scotland and his car broke down. He had no mobile phone, it was the middle of the night, he didn't have a clue what to do, but someone stopped for him, and helped make sure he was okay. He said it's scary, isn't it.

When the RAC man arrived he went through my options, but said look, I've been a mechanic for 35 years, your car won't survive this. He looked at the mileage and said 'you've done well. Most cars don't get as many miles as you've done. Later that afternoon the car was scrapped; my beautiful Fiesta, that had never even had a puncture before. I was devastated, but something within me that day was revived, because of this complete stranger, who'd seen someone had a problem and checked that I was ok and he was in no rush to drive away.

I drive a lot with my job. I'm a support worker for adults with learning disabilities. I go from house to house, helping people who need help with their medication and cooking and getting out into the community. It's a good job. It's minimum wage but I like it. I write things too. Half my life as a support worker, the other half writing. I'm always in my car or at my desk.

One of my favourite people to support is someone who is non-verbal. She lives in a supported living house with three loud men with quite severe learning disabilities and she hates it there. It's too loud for her, there are always staff having conversations, coming and going, there's too much noise. On my first day I was told she really likes going out in the car. They said you won't believe the difference, she's so anxious and tense at home, but as soon as she's out in the car she's a completely different person. They said if you're ever on shift and want to take her out, she'd love that. So that's what we do. Whenever the house gets too loud I go and fetch my car keys. There's a café we've found that we both really like. It serves good coffee for £1.30, just off the A140, and she sits there with her decaf latte.

The café always plays the same music. Instrumental versions of soul songs. It feels right that there's no lyrics, just piano. We always sit at the same table, being served by the same waitress, ordering the same drinks, going in at the same time, and I loved sitting there, both of us listening to the music. The best songs aren't complicated you can play the melody with one finger. The people I like best aren't complicated either. They reply to your texts.

The first time we went to the café I thought this would be a good opportunity to get a book out or do some writing but I realised that would be rude. It took me a while to embrace this solitude, to realise she was given me permission to zone out of life, to get away from all the noise.

March

ALL THAT GLISTERS

AND then it was Sullivan's turn to toss a fistful of dirt over the coffin. It was a gesture he never understood, but nonetheless tried his best to do well. Too soft a throw and he would appear bored, uncaring, but too hard and the margins for perceived animosity would split wide open. He had to get it right. There was a trick to it that people never talked about, a rolling in the wrist until the palm was turned up to the low sky which cracked between clouds. The earth tumbled free between his fingers. It sounded like rain on mahogany.

He didn't stay for the reception, instead popping up his umbrella and beginning the slow walk back to the train station. There was a time when Sullivan felt obliged to stay with a bereaved family until most people had gone home, but not for a little while now. Not for six months. When he stepped past the cemetery gates, he gave a single, wistful look back to the crowd gathering into the church for finger sandwiches. His stomach piped up at the thought. There was something about miniature versions of regular food that made them taste better, as if all the notes of a meal could play more delightfully upon the tongue in smaller quantities. Fumbling around in his blazer pocket, Sullivan worked his finger inside an open bag of chocolate eclairs and pulled one out. Using his teeth to pinch one end of the wrapper, he tugged it and it spun around in a blur of purple just below his range of vision. It was a poor substitute for Mrs Harrison's cream cheese and smoked salmon on white bread.

If his wife were with him, she'd tut and shake her head.

"You know those things are bad for your teeth," she'd say.

"I know, dear, but the Devil makes temptation easy and I'm a weak man." Then he'd grin and grab her waist.

"Sully! You have the appetite of a Labrador."

That was her favourite phrase. Every time he snacked between meals or went back for seconds, she told him he was behaving like a Labrador, but she'd say it with half-smile. The coy upturning of her mouth was always on the side facing away from him to hide her amusement, though he knew full well it was there and would wink in reply. After fifty years of marriage, they were bilingual; they spoke their native language and a special, coded one just for themselves.

His shoe came down in a puddle. It was just deep enough that the cold, grey water poured in over the top of his brown brogue and seeped into his argyle sock to his already numb toes beneath. Never had Sullivan wanted so desperately to be on a train, crammed into his seat next to a random, warm stranger, hurtling homeward across the drumming of steel rods. He let the remainder of the eclair slide down his throat and freed another one from the bag in his pocket. *Labrador indeed,* he thought as he popped his second sweet into his mouth. He rounded the corner and went straight through the station entrance.

The train journey was only forty-five minutes, followed by a ten minute walk. As long as there were no delays – *not bloody likely* – he'd be home within the hour. At least he was now under the cover of the station roof. Reading the screen that counted down to his train's arrival, he lowered his umbrella and shook it, before putting it into a carrier bag he'd stuffed into a pocket. Standing on the platform, Sullivan didn't see much point in searching for a spare bench upon which to park himself for the next couple of minutes – *thank God it was on time* – so instead he kept his eyes trained on the billboard behind the adjacent platform.

The woman on the advert was lifting her baby into the air, whose gleeful smile topped a chin coated in saliva and a crusting orange purée. While he sincerely believed that children were the most precious gift in the world, there was a secret he carried around since his own son, Quinn, was born; nothing was as off-putting as the bubbling, slurping mess an infant made as it ate. It was a conclusion that gathered supporting evidence over the years as Quinn grew up and moved from milk to mush. In fact, every time Sullivan ate ice cream for decades now, he couldn't help but think of Quinn's first.

Two years old was certainly too young for mini-golf, but that was the wonderful part of being a parent. Sullivan and Darleen could take little Quinn anywhere they wanted and tell people it was all for their son. They watched cartoons again, went into toy shops and played, even went to fun fairs and carnivals. Now it was mini-golf. Of course, it wasn't entirely selfish. Darleen read that children have much to gain from exposing them to lots of experiences early on – *'stimulating' was the word* – but they'd be lying if they said that it wasn't for their own enjoyment too.

After an hour of playing the course, the sun was beginning to overpower them and ice cream started to sound like the greatest idea in the world. Darleen took Quinn over to an empty field opposite to sit while Sullivan queued at the ice cream van. Over his shoulder, he watched her fan out her blue dress to the side and smooth it down, so Quinn could sit on top of it instead of directly on the grass. It was the same dress Sullivan had given her five birthdays ago and was in pristine condition, but that was typical of Darleen. She never threw out anything if it could still be saved and always took care of everyone. She wrapped an arm around Quinn and placed her hand across his tummy to support him as he leaned against her. Using her free arm to reach into their bag, she pulled out a bottle of milk and brought it up to Quinn's lips.

On his way back to them, Sullivan couldn't help but smile. The wind changed direction and brought Darleen's hair around her face and into her eyes so she couldn't see anything. It always happened and her frustration made Sullivan chuckle. In the seconds before she was able to push her hair away, Sullivan darted around behind them and tip-toed deftly, sneaking up for the perfect scare.

"Raaa!" he said as he grabbed her from behind and she shrieked.

"Sully! Jesus. Come up behind a woman alone with her baby, why don't you? That's a good way to get your eyes scratched out!"

"Come now, I've brought an icy-cold treat to placate you."

She narrowed her eyes but couldn't supress her smile as she took her ice cream from him.

"Is it working?" Sullivan asked.

"Perhaps..." she said, licking the side. Raspberry. Her favourite. "Okay. Yes. Thank you, my love. And what flavour did you get? Let me guess –"

"– Vanilla," they said together.

"It's the best one," Sullivan said.

"Best one? Don't be absurd. Vanilla isn't a proper flavour. It's the complete absence of flavour! That's the point."

"What about when you put vanilla extract in your fairy cakes? That's a flavour."

"Well...that's different, it's –"

"– oh, honey, you might want to...err..." Sullivan interrupted, pointing at her ice cream.

She turned her head to find that half of it was missing. Quinn was grinning madly beneath a pink, dripping moustache.

"Oh, you like Mummy's ice cream, do you, you little devil?" Darleen said with feigned annoyance.

Quinn giggled and leaned in for more.

Sullivan blinked as the train pulled up to the platform. His toes squelched in his damp sock as he stepped up into the carriage and made his way through the aisle, searching for a place to sit. There was only one space available that he could see. A young woman sat in the window seat on her own, staring out at the same billboard.

April

Prologue – Bang!

There was a Bang! but nobody heard it. The universe shattered but there was nobody there to see. It was tremendous. There were holes everywhere. The sky wasn't yet. There was a lot of gas. It's all so impossible to imagine let alone find the right words for. Planet earth was carved from chaos. It's been in the blood for four billion years. Continents split from the main until there was no main, rivers sprang, mountains erupted through rock, eco systems were born because weather. *Terra firma*, cluelessness, what's happening? Chaos, that's what. The dinosaurs had chaos down. I've seen the movies.

Chaos was in the bones of the first fish to walk out of the sea, it was all very nonchalant, like 'it's just me so I'll boss the joint'. But there was no joint to boss until others came in their own good time, flapped around until they had legs, stood up, pointed at something, gave it a one-syllable name. Soon after came a lot of anguish over who had the safest cave, which led to unspeakable violence. Vegetables began to grow. They changed the landscape. There were broccoli spears. Lots of men and women were fucking because it felt good. Clothing became necessary. Then more clothing as their children grew. Soon after came a lot of anguish over who had the sickest gear, which lead to unspeakable violence, and fashion.

Sun worship became necessary because life was tough and questions needed answering. Leaders rose to conduct the services; it was all very holier-than-thou. Groups formed when the priests alternately picked their favourites until it was just the dying guy at the end. They all waited until the dying guy was dead and missed him. They put a huge rock on top of his body and went their way.

Picture these cavepeople. Little heads with loping jaws. Wayward gaits. Tense fists. Intimacy was brutal. Loin cloths with crude decorations but at least something. It was a start. Faces up to the sky looking for the sun in the rain. Getting soaked. Early forms of pneumonia. More missing. More huge rocks. Bear-skinned in the glare of day, men and women picked things from the ground, had a quick bite, see if it was heading cave-wards. Some of it was rock hard and fit neatly in the palm. Exchanges of weapons. Practice on each other. Impulse control issues. Casual slaughter. Missing. Rocks. The spoils of chaos. Jealousy. Covetousness. The first side-eye. Lots of loiterers around cave entrances. The general lack of trust.

We had a vague idea of who we were, we addressed one another crudely, fair enough, it was all a very long time ago and anyway consciousness doesn't mean conscience so chaos was always close to the surface, likely to break out over the smallest of misunderstandings, like 'there wasn't enough wood for the fire' or 'it was your turn to kill the bears' or 'what are you looking at?' Rage won every day. But there was fucking every night, the desire to spread the seed a very long way down time. There were bangs and everybody heard them.

Abubelle

Observing a single day on the continent of Royy is, like a high-topped couture boot, laced with difficulty. Second-by-second social interactions grip our millions of citizens; threads of serendipity splice in the blink of an eye across our wide stretch of land, which unfurls like a tongue in a sauna, from lake to mountain, beach to forest, the climates from hot to cold and several points between. The weather can be appalling. We try to be hardy but fail. We're not the friendliest. In pettiness and violence we excel. Luckily, root vegetables are in abundance. It had been on my mind for years to take in the workings of our continent synchronically, a snapshot of time from the book of wonders I house within my comfortable existence. In short, I was after the chance to take to the skies, and once and for all look down on the men and women of Royy.

Imagine my joy when I found myself drinking with my light-aircraft-pilot friend, Ohnoo. After chatting old times when I reminded him of the photos, Ohnoo soon offered me an option to see Royy from above. It's a twin-seater, said Ohnoo, we'll need to refuel, get some decent sounds going, strap back and levitate, but I reckon we can see all Royy in the space of 24 hours. Even in the dark, Ohnoo, I said. Yes, Abubelle, he replied, that's when the fires burn brightest. When's best for you, I said, in the usual polite and undemanding manner. Any time you're ready, Abubelle, said Ohnoo, Killer Queen, my Cessna 9587dash2 is fuelled up in the car park. I made for the window because Ohnoo had drunk seven but there she was, Killer Queen, a rare aeronautical beauty amid the tired saloon cars out back.

I turned and watched Ohnoo slam his glass down on the counter and demand number eight from Dermotich the Publican. Ohnoo loves drinking whereas I'm a lightweight, only last week I dropped in on Yardburger and helped her demolish a bottle of whisky. I say help, I had a smidgeon. I say demolish, she licked the rim dry. Her skin changed colour. I spend a lot of my life surrounded by drinkers. I see a lot of skin change colour.

Come on then Ohnoo, I said, slapping his shoulders, fly me over the scalp of Royy. Show me the topsoil of our continent's daily life. Give us both a panorama to remember. Ohnoo looked at me with one eye closed, slammed his glass down, one for the air, Dermotich, he said, and leant into the wooden structure at an awkward angle. When she was sure Ohnoo wasn't watching, Dermotich shook her head. I think she wanted my attention but I was buzzing. This was the shit. I was living the dream, about to cross transnational boundaries which from 20,000 feet disappear into thin air, it's a mess of ordinance survey; anything could happen.

And for every time that truism comes true, anything did. After his fourth one for the air, Ohnoo fell from his stool and splayed on the sawdusted floor. He purged an enormous amount of liquid from his mouth. Its range was impressive. The sawdust got straight to work. There was a gash in Ohnoo's head so Dermotich came round and didn't like what she saw. That's a lot of liquid, she said, and phoned for an ambulance.

Ohnoo is still in hospital. They found several cancers. He is caught in a web of wires. I visited him. I told him how disappointed I was that his habits spoiled my dream of looking down on all Royy. He said, I'm going to be dead this time next week, Abubelle, and I said nothing but I was thinking my aerial scoop is out the window and not coming my way again any time soon, you've brought this on yourself, Ohnoo, it's no way to go around being. I then smiled easily and looked at him with my tender eyes. I attended his funeral in a pilot's suit. I wanted people to know. Killer Queen is still in the car park. Dermotich is sawing it up at the weekend.

July

FRAGMENTS

What if a woman had to save the world? What if this woman, The Saver, went to her local waste facility, and said, *these workers are human too*? What if another woman, The Finder, wants to find The Saver, but The Saver eludes her? The Finder trawls through The Saver's archive, and makes attempts to meet, but the meetings are always cancelled. What is The Saver trying to teach The Finder? At The Finder's local waste facility, they conduct tours for avid schoolkids. The kids want to make even more waste to feed the machines.

~~Don de Lillo makes statements.~~

Brushing skin flakes off the bedsheet and pillow. Whose? Hers? An absent person's? A squeezing of the bum cheeks. Retention. Stand up. The cat wanders in, ruffled and dusty. The skin flakes are not the cat's.

If we organise our waste we will be organised. Waste is the key to unlock society's ills, and assess its functionality. In *Tales of the City*, Mona assesses Mary Ann's waste and creates a portrait of the lady. Our waste profiles us. We can be subjected to a waste analysis, from which a prescription can be issued: eat less processed food, read less crap magazines; lots of vegetable peelings, good, poo is no doubt regular.

I look at *Ada* by Atak based on *Ada* by Gertrude Stein. Now I listen to Gertrude Stein read 'Matisse'. I am a cultural accumulation. I can be that. And you can be certain that you can be certain. On the cover of Akutagawa's *Rashomon and 17 Other Stories,* a toothless hag: grey hair straggles either side of the mouth and furrowed brow; wide-open eyes are circles with black pin pricks at centre. On cue, a crow. *Caw caw caw*. I return to Ada. And *Tales of the City*: fizzy-poppy-gossipy.

In 'Rashomon', the woman sits with fire on a stick. Visceral details: a pus-filled pimple. Animal analogies: he moved "with all the stealth of a lizard"; "crouched, cat-like"; a "scrawny old woman" is "white-haired and monkey-like".

Bloody nature, swollen rivers, oozing mud, gorges, adrenaline, internality, going deep inside, waste, detritus, oozing pus. The pus-filled pimple, swelling, fit to burst, to splatter, to splay its yellow pus... onto what? Onto whom? Where?

Alexander Chee writes about his time as a student of Annie Dillard in an article. Chee informs us that she would count the verbs in their manuscripts. *Bad verbs give rise to adverbs*, she would say. *Choose the right verb.*
Samuel L. Johnson was equally verb-obsessed.

Waste and the environment. The unknowableness of being alive. The race to keep up. Just as you get used to a scenario, a person, a season, an age, a weight, a height, a schedule, a political situation – things change. Life is a racing current against the tides. We are always in opposition to our decaying selves, in opposition to being one of many, in opposition to having no control of anyone or anything, including oneself. We make our comforts and distractions, our systems, our routines and rituals.

Under The Sword? A white horse gallops across the field behind the dyke. *Der Kleine Pferd*? *Der Weisse Pferd*? Stefan Zweig? Got it: *Der Schimmelreiter*, Theodor Storm.

Akutagawa's 'The Story of a Head That Fell Off ' begins with a head that knows that it is a head soon to fall off. *I'm cut, I'm cut*, he says, the voice, the consciousness that sits inside. As the head prepares to fall – at last, climax, chorus – the horse, with the head flopped over its mane, gallops across the field, the ghostly spectral presence that the rider on the white horse sees in the storm. One horse from one story jumps into another. A line is drawn. The man's head is cut. Under the line, his past – ten minutes earlier. In battle they sharpened each other's swords. We don't know this man, this warrior, in war. He was very successful.

The Making of Americans: repeating, then, is a way of repeating. Slowly, everyone comes to be clearer to someone. An ordered history of everyone. The Chinese warrior and the Japanese warrior sharpening each other's swords in the field. He was wailing, we are told, because of the dizzying ebb and flow of his emotions, centering on his fear of death. Go on existing. Family living can go on existing. They are quite certain. And anyone can come to be a dead one. A diatribe against war, and the nonsense of a man fighting a man in a field, sharpening their swords on each other, such that some can come to be dead ones. Family living. Some become dead ones. Not anyone then is remembering any such thing. Everyone is then a dead one. A diatribe against the nonsense of existing. *If I Told Him, A Completed Portrait of Picasso*. Would he like it? Xiao Er was overcome by a mysterious loneliness. Disappearing. Now all actively repeated. And do they do: A Modern Tragicomedy. Life is a modern tragicomedy. He, he, he, and he, as he, and he is, and as he is, he is and as he, and as he is, and he, and he. Oh, his head fell off, years later. He fell and hit the floor and his head fell off. A fairy tale. A modern fable. Let me recite what history teaches. And the story of the man lying in the ditch looking up at the sky, seeing mirages of home, is repeated. Retold.

A dream. Jumpers on a hill: young people, crouched like stones. I walk in a stone-walled trench. I need the toilet. *Ask the jumpers,* a girl says. I'll get them to write it on the rocks. To my left, people on a grassy bank say there's a toilet behind them. A cubicle houses a squat latrine. Dirty. Pubes. I don't go. I jump onto a two-tier display in a warehouse. I am with a man; he is looking for me.

Slipping around in the mud on the edges of the river. Feet depress sand: *schlunk, glunk.* Suction. Feet will not pull out. Panic. Hold still. Slowly pull. Leave the boots. Get to the edge. Escape the tide. The tide comes in fast. Sit now, momentarily peaceful, next to the hull of a houseboat. See how the water has pooled up behind you. You must wade now to regain the road. Heart races. Excitement. A thrill. Boots left behind. Walk barefoot along the riverside. Find a new pair of shoes: trainers slung up in a tree.

A dream. I am camping with people I don't know. I bought and then lost a coat. Now, in a shop, I find a second-hand version of the lost coat, as well as the coat I bought and lost. I try both on. It is agreed that the one I bought previously is best. We go into a field where we have each pitched a tent. A small girl lets a ball chase around a course she created. It's an artwork. This small girl is clearly Mystery from the film *Inside Out.* The girl is unhappy that I'm not more impressed by her artwork. I explain that I'm tired. The other five have put a large tent across all the small tents. I walk with some others back to my tent. It's gone. We find it pushed down a slope. We recover it and walk up to our larger encampment past a toilet tent in which four girls are using Shewees. They snarl at us. I'm with a girl with red hair in pig tails. We talk about community. *Surely it's better to embrace community, even when we're too many,* I say.

August

1. It Is Happening Again

Oh no, oh no, oh no.

That's the first thought when it starts: suddenly there, out of the blue. A presence at once menacingly unknown and sickeningly familiar. Panic number one hundred and seven. Or two. Or fifteen.

It doesn't matter the number, just that it's happening again.

2. Ten Minutes

Ten minutes.

That's how long it's going to last. At least the really bad part. The part where—even though you've been through this, or have read about it before—you aren't exactly sure what's happening. *Maybe this is something different,* the panic unhelpfully suggests.

It isn't. You are having a panic episode. It is going to last for ten minutes, and then it's going to start getting better by degrees. Here's a list of things you can do for 10 minutes:

Wash the dishes.
Fold the laundry.
Organize a cupboard.
Walk the dog.
Listen to a few of your favorite songs.
Take out the trash. And the recycling.
Walk yourself around the block.
Write.
Read.
Breathe.

I mean really you can do anything for 10 minutes if you think about it. The point is, at the end of ten minutes you are going to be two things:

1. Still alive, and
2. Feeling better.

And then 10 minutes after that, you're going to feel better still, and 10 minutes after that—a full thirty minutes after this panic tried to ruin your day—you are going to feel almost normal.

And although you were a bit beside yourself for a moment there, you'll realize that it's winding down, that the panic has left the building. Then, once you feel sure it's gone, you'll go back to feeling like you again.

And what a wonderful feeling that is, eh?

3. How Does it Feel?

How does it feel?

Symptoms caused by panicking include but are not limited to:

Rapid heartbeat
Heart palpitations
Skipped heartbeats
Dizziness
Chest pain
Having trouble breathing
Vertigo
Feeling suddenly cold
Tingling or numbness
An overwhelming feeling of doom
Sweating, cold or hot
Feeling out of body
Dissociating
Feeling like you're going to pass out
Feeling like you're losing control
Feeling like your head is on fire
Feeling a sudden heaviness
Feeling like something is wrong and you're going to die
Premonitions of catastrophe
Terror

The list could go on. If I've missed your most popular symptom, write it in the margin, or tweet them to me—I'm @seanickels.

Here's the good news: you can be experiencing any or all these symptoms and be having a panic attack instead of the big bad thing you—at this moment—think is happening. Panic is a sneaky little devil and a master of disguise; it likes to take you by surprise, dressed up as something else.

A heart attack. An aneurysm. A stroke. A brain tumor. Cancer. Spinal meningitis. MS. Schizophrenia. Parkinson's. A surreptitious and lethally venomous spider bite. An infection, beginning in that sore tooth you've had all week, that has suddenly spread—and if left untreated—will undoubtedly lead to sepsis and sudden death.

These are all costumes that panic likes to wear in order to do the thing it likes to do: scare the bejesus out of you, as my Granny used to say. I should mention that I've Googled the term symptoms of for each of the words on the above list, numerous times, and probably will do so again.

This is a bad idea.

I've found that Googling symptoms almost always fans the flames rather than puts them out. The algorithms that power these searches are trying to be helpful. They dutifully scour the internet for your search terms, which are invariably tied to one awful disease or another.

And then you have your algorithmic diagnosis:

Tumor. Not benign.

Also:

a pop-up asking you if you need help with your will.

It makes sense: panic disguises itself as other things, and so the internet thinks that your panic symptoms are heart attack symptoms, or something else.

When I feel I need to look up my symptoms, I turn to Calm Clinic's symptom list, just to remind myself that the random stabbing pain in my chest is still listed as a symptom of anxiety. It's a pretty exhaustive list, and it just helps me see this physician-compiled list of extreme ailments to remember: anxiety is a shape-shifting alien that *wants* me to think the worst. Here's that link: *https://www.calmclinic.com/category/anxiety-symptoms.*

Another strategy—for those with access, or indeed for whom this even applies—and my go-to in moments of extreme duress: call the nurse helpline on the back of your insurance card. You can tell them all the symptoms you are having, and they will give you good advice. Most likely they'll say, *well that sounds suspiciously like a panic attack.*

You can also call or text or chat with someone at a 24-hour hotline. They are staffed with volunteers, many of whom have been there (and back). The number for the American national crisis hotline is 988. It's staffed 24 hours a day, seven days a week. If you prefer to text, you can text HOME to 741741. In the UK you can dial 111 to speak with someone. And look, I know that sometimes these interactions are, erm, less than perfect (see chapter 8 for more on that) but it's quite a good thing to have somebody on the other end of the wire who might just listen.

It's a great idea to talk to someone, even if you are "just" dealing with anxiety: panic is a *real thing* that is a beast to go through alone, and bringing another human being into the equation—even if they are only on the other end of a call or a text—is often an effective way to break the hold panic tries to strangle you with.

So don't be alone. You don't have to be.

September

Points Of Interest

i. Dovestones

We make for the concrete cornerpost plughole. Whizzing across the water, backwash fizzing, breeze whispering a fresh song off the gritstone tops. Controlled havoc created without warning, we haul in and tack back towards shore. On the pier, waving… trees, sails, flags, hands. It is time, and they are waiting.

ii. Pwll Ceris

We took to sitting on the pavilion roof that summer we looked after the dog, to start with because he had a tendency to nip our ankles; later because of the view. As well as having the ideal vantage point to see the bowling green and shout down the winner of each end, we had a clear sight up the straits and out to sea. On warm nights, once the game was over and the players had packed away their woods, we'd count the starboard buoys casting their emerald glow over the left-hand side of the waters. I'm still counting.

iii. Seine

We didn't repeat what was said in the bar black with graffiti and rock posters and candle smut. It made us reckless. The stolen bottles of beer. The shoes swinging on the wire. The running from alarms. The paranoia about shadows. The weed in the river.

We lay on our backs, heads over the quayside, throats exposed, to see who gave into their stomach first. We walked the planks of barges moored with creaking lines to heavy steel rings that poison hands with the stink of old coins. We played sentry go on Pont Neuf, charging a toll to cross: a poem, a dance, a song, a sword fight.

We chatted the darkness into submission, never mentioning the thing hanging over us, then, as the pooled glass of the highest Left Bank windows coloured orange, we caught the first Métro home, and got on with the rest of our lives.

iv. The Downs

We packed away the remaining fine bone china, strapping it into the scuffed wicker basket. The blackbird became insistent, its clamour piercing the scorched evening air. Tail feathers flicked high, wings hanging beside its flanks; shirt sleeves on an untidy clothesline. Distress call better late than never.

What was it you soothed me with then? Not to worry, it's only a cup – it wasn't a full set to start with. It was once, I sighed.

We'd picked up the hamper on our travels, fashioning the occasion around the purchase, inviting our friends to join us on the heath beneath the water tower, coaxing them out of the safety of their homes and into the unwavering heat. It'll be fun, we said, a proper picnic, like in the good old days. We'll have red salmon sandwiches with cucumber and no crusts, and homemade lemon drizzle, and fizz out of flutes.

We will sit on a tartan blanket.

The ties are looser now, though there was always something missing. This just proved it; the smashing of brittle porcelain on baked ground, the breaking of the silence. Friends come and enemies go. There's always a stock needed sign in the charity shop window.

October

I want to talk, she says. Can you hear me?

I hear her faintly. I say, speak up, but I'm not sure that gets through. So I send a note, via the Author Intermediary provided when we're having these sorts of difficulties. I ask her:

What would you like to talk about?

I say it kindly. Narrators need firm kindness; otherwise they never open up, otherwise there'd be no story at all. But we must propel. Hence: firm. It would be so easy to let a thread disintegrate. I know how to do this, to coax.

She writes back. Does it matter, she writes, if I am not sure what it is yet?

Oh no, I say, because really it doesn't. Whoever knows at the beginning what it is the beginning of? Just start somewhere, I say, and I believe I hear her sigh. I believe I hear her breathe out and pick up the start of it.

Can you hear me? she says.

Yes, I say, although she is still speaking softly. We'll work on that.

I composed. A song for sitting, a song for standing. But one day I'm not sure at all how to put a note next to another note.

This doesn't seem to be the start, she says to me, and I know that a Narrator's job now is to say:

Go on.

I am alone, she says, and I want to be, although this is...

Yes?

Although this doesn't make for a good story, she says, and now I can hear her laughing. I am supposed to not want to be, she says, and there is something different in her voice. Isn't it unusual, for the heroine – I am the heroine, right? – to want to be alone? Not to be chasing someone?

Well, I say carefully, not wanting to close anything down, there are those sorts of stories.

The romantic sort, she says.

Yes, I say, quite traditional, with the desires and the thwarting of them and so on. I can hear her really laughing now. I like to hear her laugh.

What if, she says in between the giggling, I have other desires, and those get thwarted instead?

It would keep me reading, I say, although being a Narrator is a full-time job, I don't read a lot. Other stories, you know.

Ah, she says, and I can hear her louder now. Well, I think this might work then.

Go on, I say.

I am alone with my notes, and one day, there are no notes and I am alone, and so I walk.

I walk and walk, wondering to myself what kind of woman I am, this woman who had the notes and now has no notes and is putting one foot in front of another foot, trying to find the thing.

But while I walk, I am enjoying the walking, and I am not missing my notes at all, and this is not

such an interesting story, is it?

She stops. She's not laughing.

Happiness at being alone, I say carefully. There might be something in that.

Tolstoy, she says, something about all happy families being alike. He means: 'boring'.

We know about Tolstoy. As Narrators, he's caused problems. He is severe in his ideas about writing. Russians. I can see that I have to tread carefully.

Yes, I tell her, and I hear her doing something, perhaps making herself a drink. I am hoping it is only tea. I have had those problems, too. But what a challenge, I say, to try and write about the thing they insist is boring, shouldn't be written about. I am proud of myself for this one.

Oh, she says. Yes, that's a very good point.

You know, I say, I think one of the other points they make about writing is to find your voice.

I always wondered about that, she says. Surely my voice is already my voice?

This is my comfort zone, narrative voice. I know where I am here.

Yes, I say, but you don't speak in the same way to friends as you do to, say, a student in a classroom, someone in a shop. You shift and adjust your tone, your register.

True, she says. I am not talking naturally to you, for example. I don't know you. You've been assigned.

I'm here to help, I say, but I am not who you are writing for.

Ah, she says. That's the thing. What if I am writing for myself?

When we meet, the Narrators, or as many of us as can get away, in between projects or when the writers are in The Zone, as they call it, and don't need us, we discuss problems. We never get tired of talking about problems. Starting is the hardest, we tell each other. We are usually only brought in for the new ones, the ones who have never tried this before. Yes, occasionally there is an experienced one who wants to experiment and needs assistance, but much of the time, once they have two or three under their belt, they may not know how the fourth will be, but they are happy to go it alone. They know what starting is, and that they've done it.

The new ones, though, try and duck out at any opportunity. Straightjackets, we say. We've had many thoughts about innovative devices to tie them down. We have calmed each other when all we want to do is shout at our Author. A Narrator who is violent is not ideal. That's not helpful.

Endings, we say, of course. Endings are a bugger, we say, and we laugh. We laugh because there's really nothing we can do here at all. We can't put forward an ending; our guidelines are stricter about this than anything else. We can't even suggest possible avenues towards the ending. We could be struck off. It is immensely delicate.

The middle is the best part, we say to each other, opening another bag of crisps.

November

Call Centre

One day she woke up without a body. Only it wasn't really waking up, if you didn't have a body, she thought. Only it wasn't really thinking, either. But it was like waking up. That moment where you feel conscious but can't grasp the immediate past. She knew what waking up felt like because she'd had a body, once.

Once she had been a voice in an answering machine.

> Good afternoon you've reached [insert business name]. There's no one available to take your call at the moment. Please leave a message and someone will get back to you as soon as possible.

There's no one available. There is no one. Bad grammar, that, she had once thought, reading the script.

Because, once, she could read, and had been part voice, part body, part machine. Ears crushed against her head by a headset, and the wire between the headset and the monitor was an umbilical cord that was cut every evening and she was born. Or was it the spine that held together her organic and machine parts, and her voice wrapped around that cord, that spine, like flesh? Once, she didn't like it when people compared the wire to an umbilical cord or a spine. Bad metaphors, or similes, depending on if they said 'like' or not. Because once, she was not a cyborg, she was a woman in a call centre twirling the cable that ran between her headset and the monitor, and it was not umbilical or a spine, it was just a wire.

Good morning/afternoon [insert accordingly] Inga speaking, how can I help? (How *may* I help you?) I'm afraid he's out of office at the moment, can (may) I take a message and ask him to call you back? What is your name please? How do you spell that please? What company are you calling from please? Could you spell that for me please? What is your phone number please? Could you repeat that please? What is your mother's maiden name, could you spell that for me please? Do you have any allergies, what are they please? What was your worst fear as a child, could you describe that for me please? What do you feel when you look at yourself naked in the mirror, could you describe that feeling for me please? When did you last floss your teeth? What would you like me to ask you? Can you tell if I'm human or not please? I am. Not I'm (she edited the script). I am.

Once she had been unemployed, and she had told people she'd rather be on the dole than a cog in the machine. And then she was on the dole and she changed her mind. Bouncing payments and pot noodle, ketchup sandwiches made from stolen sachets; cards declined and meter keys with blinking lights; sellotaping the letterbox shut only to find the waves of envelopes lapping at the other side of the door, and wading through them in the hallway in wellingtons, and that was more embarrassing than removing the Sellotape. And the letters always said Dear Inga, and always spelled her surname wrong.

Once she had been a teenage girl with too much pocket money and picked pockets anyway. Or not enough pocket money, or none, or had been raised by au pairs, or had this or that or the other kind of childhood.

Once she had been caught drinking sea water, it tasted good and she had wet sand stuck to burnt skin, cold wind blew burning, and the water tasted like olives and the smell of seaweed, she had shiny blue nail varnish on her toenails, sand-scraped, and broken shells she had skin she had a body. Once. But. Once she had woken up, once she was without a body, and couldn't wake up and couldn't sleep in a paper tent to cover her, otherwise naked beneath the baking thirsty sun she could not burn, she could not taste sea water anymore.

Direct Marketing

Duncan was interviewed in the basement of a converted townhouse in the city centre. He sat opposite a panel of three people. The man on the panel was wearing a suit that looked like his, bought in Primark. The two women were wearing strong perfume and one woman had lip-gloss that made little strings between her upper and lower lip when her mouth was partly open, as she wrote things down. She didn't ask him anything. She just took notes. The other woman was in charge. She spent the interview leaning towards him with her hands clasped on the table, looking straight at him. Whenever he looked away and back again, she was looking at him. The man asked him if he felt that he had leadership qualities, if he had ambitions to manage his own team one day. Duncan said yes. She asked him where he saw himself in five years' time. He said, sitting in your seat. They looked impressed. They asked what his strengths and weaknesses were. He said his strength was team leadership and his weakness was obsessive attention to detail. The other woman continued taking notes.

They told him that every member of staff that they hired had the fantastic opportunity to become the manager of the next branch that they were opening. They preferred people with no experience. That way, they could train them according to the company standards without coming up against any bad sales habits. They told him the role was Direct Marketing. Nothing like door-to-door sales. No. That was a thing of the past. Direct Marketing meant bringing the product to the potential client, and developing a face-to-face connection with them. There was quick career progression. Competitive pay meant that the job was commission only. There was no basic pay. They found that people worked harder and produced better results when this safety net wasn't holding them back. There were also prizes if you sold lots of things. First, you had to prove that you had NSF – Natural Sales Flair.

They called Duncan the day after the interview to say that, after much consideration, he was one of the lucky few that had made it to the next stage. At the training and assessment day, they took him out on a job so that he could observe and learn from one of the senior Direct Marketers in action. He met Rory outside the building where he'd had his interview. Rory was wearing a Primark suit like him, and like the man on the interview panel. Rory had cufflinks with pearls on them. He was saving up for his wedding, and had won several prizes at work, including a flat screen TV. They walked from the building to the bus stop and waited, while Rory told him that the company had changed his life, and that he had started right at the bottom and worked his way up. Everybody did. It was all based on how good you were at Direct Marketing, nothing else mattered.

It started snowing. They got on the bus to Castlemilk shopping centre, and he asked Rory what happened if no one bought anything. Rory said that of course it wouldn't make sense for the comany to pay them unless they were making sales. Today Duncan would watch Rory selling meter keys. These keys were a fantastic deal, Rory said, a total bargain. Usually, a big electric company charged a flat daily rate on their meter key and would charge extra if you used more electricity than they deemed standard. So you were being charged for electricity even if you didn't use any. This meter key was pay-as-you-go, but with no flat rate. You only paid for what you used, at a slightly higher rate than the big companies, sure, but only for what you used.

They got off at the shopping centre and sat down in the Greggs, where Rory gave him some paperwork to fill in. Rory treated him to a cup of tea and a sausage roll. Duncan ticked the relevant Equal Opportunities boxes, and wrote down his personal details. He wrote long answers to questions about why he was perfect for the role. As he wiped crumbs off the forms, they left little stains of grease on the paper.

Then Rory asked him to stand beside him at the entrance of the shopping centre and observe his technique. It was a Tuesday morning. No one came in or out. Rory straightened his tie. He held a clipboard in one arm, and a meter key in his other hand. After a while, Rory began swinging the meter key on its keyring, round and around his finger. They walked up and down in front of the entrance. The automatic entrance doors opened and closed as they walked, and flurries of snow drifted in.

December

That we will believe *again* rather than *still.*

That we would be capable of answering with a single word.

That our lacks would always lack us.

That our mother would appear in a dream not shadowy, or hidden, but wholly there, addressing us.

That the plant we cut from her plant would grow more quickly.

That we will, as a way to stop thinking, become mystics.

That we will not become mystics.

That we would fuss with the Gordian knot rather than cut it.

That the falling light outside will not fall in us.

That the second-hand could stick.

That set dressers would not fill drawers whose insides the audience cannot see.

That the conditions will never be *just right.*

That we will not ask for yet another voice, in case it proliferates.

That the industrial bakery with its scent would be closer.

That Montaigne would at least once mention his mother.

That the asymmetry of others' faces in mirrors would not be metaphysically jarring.

That we will discard anything with more than one unintentional hole in.

That it would be possible to say *No, I have not read Wittgenstein.*

That we will hear tick-tock for what it really is: tick-tick.

That fewer things will be glossy.

That we will not feel thirsty merely because we don't have a drink.

That we will laugh less ostentatiously when we don't understand the joke.

That someone would say *Take a lot: take two.*

That the finished would not always be inferior to the un-.

That night thought would weigh the same as morning thought.

That the rest of the orchestra will always be busy with its own playing.

That when someone hasn't heard what we've said and asks us to repeat it we'll repeat it without changing a word.

That Hamlet's best audience would not be himself.

That we will know the date, as a matter of course.

That not using our faults will not cause us to forget we have them.

That diaristic writing would not always be working secretly on behalf of the past.

That people would *believe it* when thanked.

That we could answer any question to which we knew the answer.

That we will scratch *nothing*.

That churches would not have *For Sale* signs on them.

That we could find a useable synonym for *hello*.

That we will not cry about someone's predicament in front of the person whose predicament it is.

That we will crouch in the kitchen to look at the snail's moonlit tracks.

That peace would not depend entirely on the ability to suffer well.

That our inherited aneurysm won't rupture.

That our grandmother will think of her daughter hardly ever.

That *psyche* will again be a translation of *soul*.

That ceilings will continue, when stared at long enough, to appear to be their own rooms.

That we will not feel guilty turning plants around when they grow lopsidedly towards the sun.

That the orange candle we bought when we moved out will always have that sharp reminding holiday stink.

That we will never fall below nine and a half stone.

That we will not be the compass of our own seas.

That we will say words now and again merely for their sound, but not in public.

That we will not suffer any more epiphanies.

That every reading would not be a first reading.

That we could love someone without pitying their childhood.

That the present would not fill out only in remembrance.

That the blue sky will continue to demand new descriptions for itself.

That the world would not begin talking only after we're in the hallway, coat on.

That our happiness for others' happiness would last longer.

That we will wish people Merry Christmas first.

That gallery and museum visitors would not walk with that strange obsequious stoop.

That flirting would continue to be the basis of friendship.

That we will be pitied only when trying to be pitiful.

That we could always see the difference between refining and blunting.

5 years later, we're still laying out our unrest

www.ingramcontent.com/pod-product-compliance
Lightning Source LLC
Chambersburg PA
CBHW030818090426
42737CB00009B/779
* 9 7 8 1 9 1 5 0 7 9 7 7 0 *